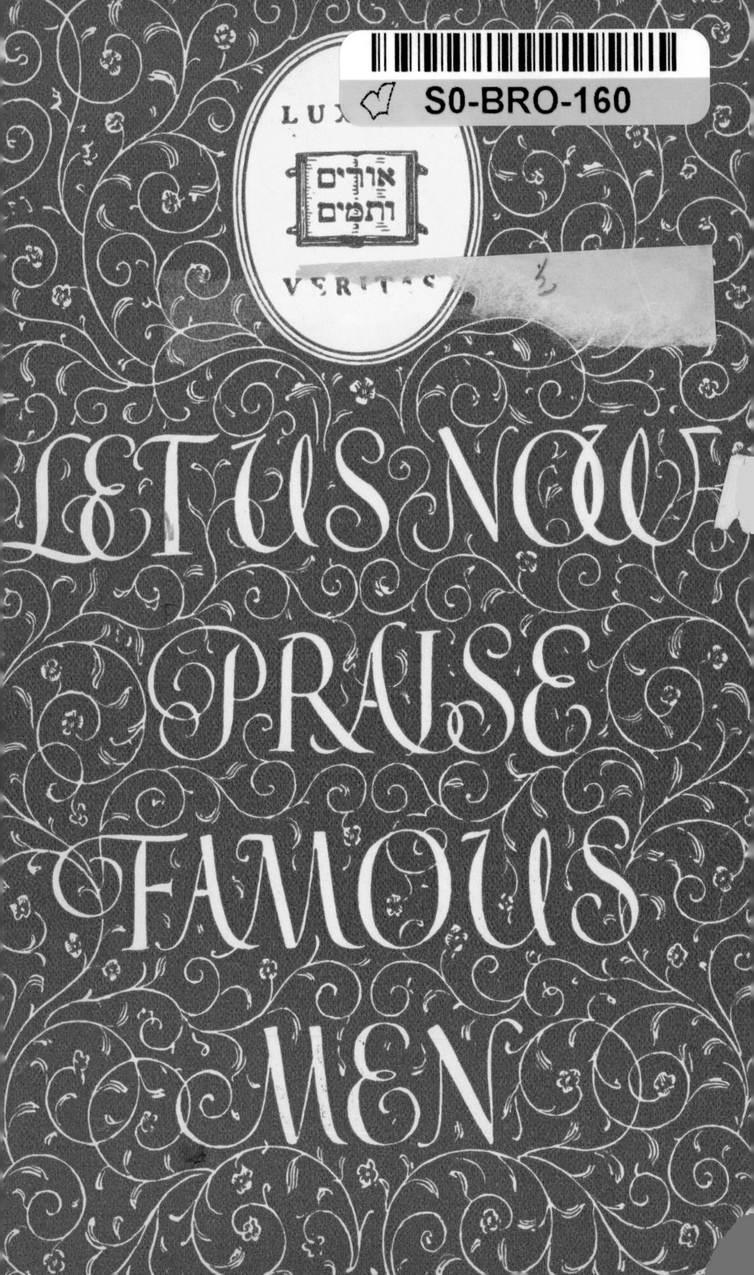
S0-BRO-160
LUX
VERITAS
LET US NOW
PRAISE
FAMOUS
MEN

THE HISPANIC NATIONS OF THE NEW WORLD

TEXTBOOK EDITION

∴

THE CHRONICLES OF AMERICA SERIES

ALLEN JOHNSON
EDITOR

GERHARD R. LOMER
CHARLES W. JEFFERYS
ASSISTANT EDITORS

THE LAST MOMENTS OF MAXIMILIAN
After the painting by Jean Paul Laurens

THE HISPANIC NATIONS OF THE NEW WORLD

A CHRONICLE OF OUR SOUTHERN NEIGHBORS

BY WILLIAM R. SHEPHERD

NEW HAVEN: YALE UNIVERSITY PRESS
TORONTO: GLASGOW, BROOK & CO.
LONDON: HUMPHREY MILFORD
OXFORD UNIVERSITY PRESS
1921

CONTENTS

ILLUSTRATIONS

THE HISPANIC NATIONS OF THE NEW WORLD

CHAPTER I

THE HERITAGE FROM SPAIN AND PORTUGAL

At the time of the American Revolution most of the New World still belonged to Spain and Portugal, whose captains and conquerors had been the first to come to its shores. Spain had the lion's share, but Portugal held Brazil, in itself a vast land of unsuspected resources. No empire mankind had ever yet known rivaled in size the illimitable domains of Spain and Portugal in the New World; and none displayed such remarkable contrasts in land and people. Boundless plains and forests, swamps and deserts, mighty mountain chains, torrential streams and majestic rivers, marked the surface of the country. This vast territory stretched from the temperate prairies west of the Mississippi down to the steaming lowlands of Central America, then up through tablelands in the southern continent to high plateaus, miles above sea level, where the sun blazed and the cold, dry air was hard to breathe, and then higher still to the lofty peaks of the Andes, clad in eternal snow or pouring fire and smoke from their summits in the clouds, and thence to the lower temperate valleys, grassy pampas, and undulating hills of the far south.

Scattered over these vast colonial domains in the Western World were somewhere between 12,000,000 and 19,000,000 people subject to Spain, and perhaps 3,000,000, to Portugal; the great majority of them were Indians and negroes, the latter predominating in the lands bordering on the Caribbean Sea and along the shores of Brazil. Possibly one-fourth of the inhabitants came of European stock, including not only Spaniards and their descendants but also the folk who spoke English in the Floridas and French in Louisiana.

During the centuries which had elapsed since the entry of the Spaniards and Portuguese into these regions an extraordinary fusion of races had taken place. White, red, and black had mingled to such an extent that the bulk of the settled population became half-caste. Only in the more temperate regions of the far north and south, where the aborigines were comparatively few or had disappeared altogether, did the whites remain racially distinct. Socially the Indian and the negro counted for little. They constituted the laboring class on whom all the burdens fell and for whom advantages in the body politic were scant. Legally the Indian under Spanish rule stood on a footing of equality with his white fellows, and many a gifted native came to be reckoned a force in the community, though his social position remained a subordinate one. Most of the negroes were slaves and were more kindly treated by the Spaniards than by the Portuguese.

Though divided among themselves, the Europeans were everywhere politically dominant. The Spaniard was always an individualist. Besides, he often brought from the Old World petty provincial traditions which were intensified in the New. The inhabitants of towns, many of which had been founded quite independently of one another, knew little about their remote neighbors and often were quite willing to convert their ignorance into prejudice. The dweller in the uplands and the resident on the coast were wont to view each other with disfavor. The one was thought heavy and stupid, the other frivolous and lazy. Native Spaniards regarded the Creoles, or American born, as persons who had degenerated more or less by their contact with the aborigines and the wilderness. For their part, the Creoles looked upon the Spaniards as upstarts and intruders, whose sole claim to consideration lay in the privileges dispensed them by the home government. In testimony of this attitude they coined for their oversea kindred numerous nicknames which were more expressive than complimentary. While the Creoles held most of the wealth and of the lower offices, the Spaniards enjoyed the perquisites and emoluments of the higher posts.

Though objects of disdain to both these masters, the Indians generally preferred the Spaniard to the Creole. The Spaniard represented a distant authority interested in the welfare of its humbler subjects and came less into actual daily contact with the natives. While it would hardly be correct to say that the Spaniard was viewed as a protector and the Creole as an oppressor, yet the aborigines unconsciously made some such hazy distinction — if indeed they did not view all Europeans with suspicion and dislike. In Brazil the relation of classes was much the same, except that here the native element was much less conspicuous as a social factor.

These distinctions were all the more accentuated by the absence both of other European peoples and of a definite middle class of any race. Everywhere in the areas tenanted originally by Spaniards and Portuguese the European of alien stock was unwelcome, even though he obtained a grudging permission from the home governments to remain a colonist. In Brazil, owing to the close commercial connections between Great Britain and Portugal, foreigners were not so rigidly excluded as in Spanish America. The Spaniard was unwilling that lands so rich in natural treasures should be thrown open to exploitation by others, even if the newcomer professed the Catholic faith. The heretic was denied admission as a matter of course. Had the foreigner been allowed to enter, the risk of such exploitation doubtless would have been increased, but a middle class might have arisen to weld the discordant factions into a society which had common desires and aspirations. With the development of commerce and industry, with the growth of activities which bring men into touch with each other in everyday affairs, something like a solidarity of sentiment might have been awakened. In its absence the only bond among the dominant whites was their sense of superiority to the colored masses beneath them.

Manual labor and trade had never attracted the Spaniards and the Portuguese. The army, the church, and the law were the three callings that offered the greatest opportunity for distinction. Agriculture, grazing, and mining they did not disdain, provided that superintendence and not actual work was the main requisite. The economic organization which the Spaniards and Portuguese established in America was naturally a more or less faithful reproduction of that to which they had been accustomed at home. Agriculture and grazing became the chief occupations. Domestic animals and many kinds of plants brought from Europe throve wonderfully in their new home. Huge estates were the rule; small farms, the exception. On the ranches and plantations vast droves of cattle, sheep, and horses were raised, as well as immense crops. Mining, once so much in vogue, had become an occupation of secondary importance.

On their estates the planter, the ranchman, and the mine owner lived like feudal overlords, waited upon by Indian and negro peasants who also tilled the fields, tended the droves, and dug the earth for precious metals and stones. Originally the natives had been forced to work under conditions approximating actual servitude, but gradually the harsher features of this system had given way to a mode of service closely resembling peonage. Paid a pitifully small wage, provided with a hut of reeds or sun-dried mud and a tiny patch of soil on which to grow a few hills of the corn and beans that were his usual nourishment, the ordinary Indian or half-caste laborer was scarcely more than a beast of burden, a creature in whom civic virtues of a high order were not likely to develop. If he betook himself to the town his possible usefulness lessened in proportion as he fell into drunken or dissolute habits, or lapsed into a state of lazy and vacuous dreaminess, enlivened only by chatter or the rolling of a cigarette. On the other hand, when employed in a capacity where native talent might be tested, he often revealed a power of action which, if properly guided, could be turned to excellent account. As a cowboy, for example, he became a capital horseman, brave, alert, skillful, and daring.

Commerce with Portugal and Spain was long confined to yearly fairs and occasional trading fleets that plied between fixed points. But when liberal decrees threw open numerous ports in the mother countries to traffic and the several colonies were given also the privilege of exchanging their products among themselves, the volume of exports and imports increased and gave an impetus to activity which brought a notable release from the torpor and vegetation characterizing earlier days. Yet, even so, communication was difficult and irregular. By sea the distances were great and the vessels slow. Overland the natural obstacles to transportation were so numerous and the methods of conveyance so cumbersome and expensive that the people of one province were practically strangers to their neighbors.

Matters of the mind and of the soul were under the guardianship of the Church. More than merely a spiritual mentor, it controlled education and determined in large measure the course of intellectual life. Possessed of vast wealth in lands and revenues, its monasteries and priories, its hospitals and asylums, its residences of ecclesiastics, were the finest buildings in every community, adorned with the masterpieces of sculptors and painters. A village might boast of only a few squalid huts, yet there in the "plaza," or central square, loomed up a massively imposing edifice of worship, its towers pointing heavenward, the sign and symbol of triumphant power.

The Church, in fact, was the greatest civilizing agency that Spain and Portugal had at their disposal. It inculcated a reverence for the monarch and his ministers and fostered a deep-rooted sentiment of conservatism which made disloyalty and innovation almost sacrilegious. In the Spanish colonies in particular the Church not only protected the natives against the rapacity of many a white master but taught them the rudiments of the Christian faith, as well as useful arts and trades. In remote places, secluded so far as possible from contact with Europeans, missionary pioneers gathered together groups of neophytes whom they rendered docile and industrious, it is true, but whom they often deprived of initiative and self-reliance and kept illiterate and superstitious.

Education was reserved commonly for members of the ruling class. As imparted in the universities and schools, it savored strongly of medievalism. Though some attention was devoted to the natural sciences, experimental methods were not encouraged and found no place in lectures and textbooks. Books, periodicals, and other publications came under ecclesiastical inspection, and a vigilant censorship determined what was fit for the public to read.

Supreme over all the colonial domains was the government of their majesties, the monarchs of Spain and Portugal. A ministry and a council managed the affairs of the inhabitants of America and guarded their destinies in accordance with the theories of enlightened despotism then prevailing in Europe. The Spanish dominions were divided into viceroyalties and subdivided into captaincies general, presidencies, and intendancies. Associated with the high officials who ruled them were *audiencias*, or boards, which were at once judicial and administrative. Below these individuals and bodies were a host of lesser functionaries who, like their superiors, held their posts by appointment. In Brazil the governor general bore the title of viceroy and carried on the administration assisted by provincial captains, supreme courts, and local officers.

This control was by no means so autocratic as it might seem. Portugal had too many interests elsewhere, and was too feeble besides, to keep tight rein over a territory so vast and a population so much inclined as the Brazilian to form itself into provincial units, jealous of the central authority.

Spain, on its part, had always practised the good old Roman rule of "divide and govern." Its policy was to hold the balance among officials, civil and ecclesiastical, and inhabitants, white and colored. It knew how strongly individualistic the Spaniard was and realized the full force of the adage, "I obey, but I do not fulfill!" Legislatures and other agencies of government directly representative of the people did not exist in Spanish or Portuguese America. The Spanish *cabildo*, or town council, however, afforded an opportunity for the expression of the popular will and often proved intractable. Its membership was appointive, elective, hereditary, and even purchasable, but the form did not affect the substance. The Spanish Americans had an instinct for politics. "Here all men govern," declared one of the viceroys; "the people have more part in political discussions than in any other provinces in the world; a council of war sits in every house."

CHAPTER II

"OUR OLD KING OR NONE"

THE movement which led eventually to the emancipation of the colonies differed from the local uprisings which occurred in various parts of South America during the eighteenth century. Either the arbitrary conduct of individual governors or excessive taxation had caused the earlier revolts. To the final revolution foreign nations and foreign ideas gave the necessary impulse. A few members of the intellectual class had read in secret the writings of French and English philosophers. Others had traveled abroad and came home to whisper to their countrymen what they had seen and heard in lands more progressive than Spain and Portugal. The commercial relations, both licit and illicit, which Great Britain had maintained with several of the colonies had served to diffuse among them some notions of what went on in the busy world outside.

By gaining its independence, the United States had set a practical example of what might be done elsewhere in America. Translated into French, the Declaration of Independence was read and commented upon by enthusiasts who dreamed of the possibility of applying its principles in their own lands. More powerful still were the ideas liberated by the French Revolution and Napoleon. Borne across the ocean, the doctrines of "Liberty, Fraternity, Equality" stirred the ardent-minded to thoughts of action, though the Spanish and Portuguese Americans who schemed and plotted were the merest handful. The seed they planted was slow to germinate among peoples who had been taught to regard things foreign as outlandish and heretical. Many years therefore elapsed before the ideas of the few became the convictions of the masses, for the conservatism and loyalty of the common people were unbelievably steadfast.

Not Spanish and Portuguese America, but Santo Domingo, an island which had been under French rule since 1795 and which was tenanted chiefly by ignorant and brutalized negro slaves, was the scene of the first effectual assertion of independence in the lands originally colonized by Spain. Rising in revolt against their masters, the negroes had won complete control under their remarkable commander, Toussaint L'Ouverture, when Napoleon Bonaparte, then First Consul, decided to restore the old régime. But the huge expedition which was sent to reduce the island ended in absolute failure. After a ruthless racial warfare, characterized by ferocity on both sides, the French retired. In 1804 the negro leaders proclaimed the independence of the island as the "Republic of Haiti," under a President who, appreciative of the example just set by Napoleon, informed his followers that he too had assumed the august title of "Emperor"! His immediate successor in African royalty was the notorious Henri Christophe, who gathered about him a nobility garish in color and taste — including their sable lordships, the "Duke of Marmalade" and the "Count of Lemonade"; and who built the palace of "Sans Souci" and the countryseats of "Queen's Delight" and "King's Beautiful View," about which cluster tales of barbaric pleasure that rival the grim legends clinging to the parapets and enshrouding the dungeons of his mountain fortress of "La Ferrière." None of these black or mulatto potentates, however, could expel French authority from the eastern part of Santo Domingo. That task was taken in hand by the inhabitants themselves, and in 1809 they succeeded in restoring the control of Spain.

Meanwhile events which had been occurring in South America prepared the way for the movement that was ultimately to banish the flags of both Spain and Portugal from the continents of the New World. As the one country had fallen more or less under the influence of France, so the other had become practically dependent upon Great Britain. Interested in the expansion of its commerce and viewing the outlying possessions of peoples who submitted to French guidance as legitimate objects for seizure, Great Britain in 1797 wrested Trinidad from the feeble grip of Spain and thus acquired a strategic position very near South America itself. Haiti, Trinidad, and Jamaica, in fact, all became centers of revolutionary agitation and havens of refuge for Spanish American radicals in the troublous years to follow.

Foremost among the early conspirators was the Venezuelan, Francisco de Miranda, known to his fellow Americans of Spanish stock as the "Precursor." Napoleon once remarked of him: "He is a Don Quixote, with this difference — he is not crazy. . . . The man has sacred fire in his soul."

An officer in the armies of Spain and of revolutionary France and later a resident of London, Miranda devoted thirty years of his adventurous life to the cause of independence for his countrymen. With officials of the British Government he labored long and zealously, eliciting from them vague promises of armed support and some financial aid. It was in London, also, that he organized a group of sympathizers into the secret society called the "Grand Lodge of America." With it, or with its branches in France and Spain, many of the leaders of the subsequent revolution came to be identified.

In 1806, availing himself of the negligence of the United States and having the connivance of the British authorities in Trinidad, Miranda headed two expeditions to the coast of Venezuela. He had hoped that his appearance would be the signal for a general uprising; instead, he was treated with indifference. His countrymen seemed to regard him as a tool of Great Britain, and no one felt disposed to accept the blessings of liberty under that guise. Humiliated, but not despairing, Miranda returned to London to await a happier day.

Two British expeditions which attempted to conquer the region about the Rio de la Plata in 1806 and 1807 were also frustrated by this same stubborn loyalty. When the Spanish viceroy fled, the inhabitants themselves rallied to the defense of the country and drove out the invaders. Thereupon the people of Buenos Aires, assembled in *cabildo abierto*, or town meeting, deposed the viceroy and chose their victorious leader in his stead until a successor could be regularly appointed.

Then, in 1808, fell the blow which was to shatter the bonds uniting Spain to its continental dominions in America. The discord and corruption which prevailed in that unfortunate country afforded Napoleon an opportunity to oust its feeble king and his incompetent son, Ferdinand, and to place Joseph Bonaparte on the throne. But the master of Europe underestimated the fighting ability of Spaniards. Instead of humbly complying with his mandate, they rose in arms against the usurper and created a central junta, or revolutionary committee, to govern in the name of Ferdinand VII, as their rightful ruler.

The news of this French aggression aroused in the colonies a spirit of resistance as vehement as that in the mother country. Both Spaniards and Creoles repudiated the "intruder king." Believing, as did their comrades oversea, that Ferdinand was a helpless victim in the hands of Napoleon, they recognized the revolutionary government and sent great sums of money to Spain to aid in the struggle against the French. Envoys from Joseph Bonaparte seeking an acknowledgment of his rule were angrily rejected and were forced to leave.

The situation on both sides of the ocean was now an extraordinary one. Just as the junta in Spain had no legal right to govern, so the officials in the colonies, holding their posts by appointment from a deposed king, had no legal authority, and the people would not allow them to accept new commissions from a usurper. The Church, too, detesting Napoleon as the heir of a revolution that had undermined the Catholic faith and regarding him as a godless despot who had made the Pope a captive, refused to recognize the French pretender. Until Ferdinand VII could be restored to his throne, therefore, the colonists had to choose whether they would carry on the administration under the guidance of the self-constituted authorities in Spain, or should themselves create similar organizations in each of the colonies to take charge of affairs. The former course was favored by the official element and its supporters among the conservative classes, the latter by the liberals, who felt that they had as much right as the people of the mother country to choose the form of government best suited to their interests.

Each party viewed the other with distrust. Opposition to the more democratic procedure, it was felt, could mean nothing less than secret submission to the pretensions of Joseph Bonaparte; whereas the establishment in America of any organizations like those in Spain surely indicated a spirit of disloyalty toward Ferdinand VII himself. Under circumstances like these, when the junta and its successor, the council of regency, refused to make substantial concessions to the colonies, both parties were inevitably drifting toward independence. In the phrase of Manuel Belgrano, one of the great leaders in the viceroyalty of La Plata, "our old King or none" became the watchword that gradually shaped the thoughts of Spanish Americans.

When, therefore, in 1810, the news came that the French army had overrun Spain, democratic ideas so long cherished in secret and propagated so industriously by Miranda and his followers at last found expression in a series of uprisings in the four viceroyalties of La Plata, Peru, New Granada, and New Spain. But in each of these viceroyalties the revolution ran a different course. Sometimes it was the capital city that led off; sometimes a provincial town; sometimes a group of individuals in the country districts. Among the actual participants in the various movements very little harmony was to be found. Here a particular leader claimed obedience; there a board of self-chosen magistrates held sway; elsewhere a town or province refused to acknowledge the central authority. To add to these complications, in 1812, a revolutionary Cortes, or legislative body, assembled at Cadiz, adopted for Spain and its dominions a constitution providing for direct representation of the colonies in oversea administration. Since arrangements of this sort contented many of the Spanish Americans who had protested against existing abuses, they were quite unwilling to press their grievances further. Given all these evidences of division in activity and counsel, one does not find it difficult to foresee the outcome.

On May 25, 1810, popular agitation at Buenos Aires forced the Spanish viceroy of La Plata to resign. The central authority was thereupon vested in an elected junta that was to govern in the name of Ferdinand VII. Opposition broke out immediately. The northern and eastern parts of the viceroyalty showed themselves quite unwilling to obey these upstarts. Meantime, urged on by radicals who revived the Jacobin doctrines of revolutionary France, the junta strove to suppress in rigorous fashion any symptoms of disaffection; but it could do nothing to stem the tide of separation in the rest of the viceroyalty — in Charcas (Bolivia), Paraguay, and the Banda Oriental, or East Bank, of the Uruguay.

At Buenos Aires acute difference of opinion — about the extent to which the movement should be carried and about the permanent form of government to be adopted as well as the method of establishing it — produced a series of political commotions little short of anarchy. Triumvirates followed the junta into power; supreme directors alternated with triumvirates; and constituent assemblies came and went. Under one authority or another the name of the viceroyalty was changed to "United Provinces of La Plata River"; a seal, a flag, and a coat of arms were chosen; and numerous features of the Spanish régime were abolished, including titles of nobility, the Inquisition, the slave trade, and restrictions on the press. But so chaotic were the conditions within and so disastrous the campaigns without, that eventually commissioners were sent to Europe, bearing instructions to seek a king for the distracted country.

When Charcas fell under the control of the viceroy of Peru, Paraguay set up a régime for itself. At Asunción, the capital, a revolutionary outbreak in 1811 replaced the Spanish intendant by a triumvirate, of which the most prominent member was Dr. José Gaspar Rodríguez de Francia. A lawyer by profession, familiar with the history of Rome, an admirer of France and Napoleon, a misanthrope and a recluse, possessing a blind faith in himself and actuated by a sense of implacable hatred for all who might venture to thwart his will, this extraordinary personage speedily made himself master of the country. A population composed chiefly of Indians, docile in temperament and submissive for many years to the paternal rule of Jesuit missionaries, could not fail to become pliant instruments in his hands. At his direction, therefore, Paraguay declared itself independent of both Spain and La Plata. This done, an obedient Congress elected Francia consul of the republic and later invested him with the title of dictator. In the Banda Oriental two distinct movements appeared. Montevideo, the capital, long a center of royalist sympathies and for some years hostile to the revolutionary government in Buenos Aires, was reunited with La Plata in 1814. Elsewhere the people of the province followed the fortunes of José Gervasio Artigas, an able and valiant cavalry officer, who roamed through it at will, bidding defiance to any authority not his own. Most of the former viceroyalty of La Plata had thus, to all intents and purposes, thrown off the yoke of Spain.

Chile was the only other province that for a while gave promise of similar action. Here again it was the capital city that took the lead. On receipt of the news of the occurrences at Buenos Aires in May, 1810, the people of Santiago forced the captain general to resign and, on the 18th of September, replaced him by a junta of their own choosing. But neither this body, nor its successors, nor even the Congress that assembled the following year, could establish a permanent and effective government. Nowhere in Spanish America, perhaps, did the lower classes count for so little, and the upper class for so much, as in Chile. Though the great landholders were disposed to favor a reasonable amount of local autonomy for the country, they refused to heed the demands of the radicals for complete independence and the establishment of a republic. Accordingly, in proportion as their opponents resorted to measures of compulsion, the gentry gradually withdrew their support and offered little resistance when troops dispatched by the viceroy of Peru restored the Spanish régime in 1814. The irreconcilable among the patriots fled over the Andes to the western part of La Plata, where they found hospitable refuge.

But of all the Spanish dominions in South America none witnessed so desperate a struggle for emancipation as the viceroyalty of New Granada. Learning of the catastrophe that had befallen the mother country, the leading citizens of Caracas, acting in conjunction with the *cabildo*, deposed the captain general on April 19, 1810, and created a junta in his stead. The example was quickly followed by most of the smaller divisions of the province. Then when Miranda returned from England to head the revolutionary movement, a Congress, on July 5, 1811, declared Venezuela independent of Spain. Carried away, also, by the enthusiasm of the moment, and forgetful of the utter unpreparedness of the country, the Congress promulgated a federal constitution modeled on that of the United States, which set forth all the approved doctrines of the rights of man.

Neither Miranda nor his youthful coadjutor,

Simón Bolívar, soon to become famous in the annals of Spanish American history, approved of this plunge into democracy. Ardent as their patriotism was, they knew that the country needed centralized control and not experiments in confederation or theoretical liberty. They speedily found out, also, that they could not count on the support of the people at large. Then, almost as if Nature herself disapproved of the whole proceeding, a frightful earthquake in the following year shook many a Venezuelan town into ruins. Everywhere the royalists took heart. Dissensions broke out between Miranda and his subordinates. Betrayed into the hands of his enemies, the old warrior himself was sent away to die in a Spanish dungeon. And so the "earthquake" republic collapsed.

But the rigorous measures adopted by the royalists to sustain their triumph enabled Bolívar to renew the struggle in 1813. He entered upon a campaign which was signalized by acts of barbarity on both sides. His declaration of "war to the death" was answered in kind. Wholesale slaughter of prisoners, indiscriminate pillage, and wanton destruction of property spread terror and desolation throughout the country. Acclaimed "Liberator of Venezuela" and made dictator by the people of Caracas, Bolívar strove in vain to overcome the half-savage *llaneros*, or cowboys of the plains, who despised the innovating aristocrats of the capital. Though he won a few victories, he did not make the cause of independence popular, and, realizing his failure, he retired into New Granada.

In this region an astounding series of revolutions and counter-revolutions had taken place. Unmindful of pleas for coöperation, the Creole leaders in town and district, from 1810 onward, seized control of affairs in a fashion that betokened a speedy disintegration of the country. Though the viceroy was deposed and a general Congress was summoned to meet at the capital, Bogotá, efforts at centralization encountered opposition in every quarter. Only the royalists managed to preserve a semblance of unity. Separate republics sprang into being and in 1813 declared their independence of Spain. Presidents and congresses were pitted against one another. Towns fought among themselves. Even parishes demanded local autonomy. For a while the services of Bolívar were invoked to force rebellious areas into obedience to the principle of confederation, but with scant result. Unable to agree with his fellow officers and displaying traits of moral weakness which at this time as on previous occasions showed that he had not yet risen to a full sense of responsibility, the Liberator renounced the task and fled to Jamaica.

The scene now shifts northward to the viceroyalty of New Spain. Unlike the struggles already described, the uprisings that began in 1810 in central Mexico were substantially revolts of Indians and half-castes against white domination. On the 16th of September, a crowd of natives rose under the leadership of Miguel Hidalgo, a parish priest of the village of Dolores. Bearing on their banners the slogan, "Long live Ferdinand VII and down with bad government," the undisciplined crowd, soon to number tens of thousands, aroused such terror by their behavior that the whites were compelled to unite in self-defense. It mattered not whether Hidalgo hoped to establish a republic or simply to secure for his followers relief from oppression: in either case the whites could expect only Indian domination. Before the trained forces of the whites a horde of natives, so ignorant of modern warfare that some of them tried to stop cannon balls by clapping their straw hats over the mouths of the guns, could not stand their ground. Hidalgo was captured and shot, but he was succeeded by José María Morelos, also a priest. Reviving the old Aztec name for central Mexico, he summoned a "Congress of Anáhuac," which in 1813 asserted that dependence on the throne of Spain was "forever broken and dissolved." Abler and more humane than Hidalgo, he set up a revolutionary government that the authorities of Mexico failed for a while to suppress.

In 1814, therefore, Spain still held the bulk of its dominions. Trinidad, to be sure, had been lost to Great Britain, and both Louisiana and West Florida to the United States. Royalist control, furthermore, had ceased in parts of the viceroyalties of La Plata and New Granada. To regain Trinidad and Louisiana was hopeless; but a wise policy of conciliation or an overwhelming display of armed force might yet restore Spanish rule where it had been merely suspended.

Very different was the course of events in Brazil. Strangely enough, the first impulse toward independence was given by the Portuguese royal family. Terrified by the prospective invasion of the country by a French army, late in 1807 the Prince Regent, the royal family, and a host of Portuguese nobles and commoners took passage on British vessels and sailed to Rio de Janeiro. Brazil thereupon became the seat of royal government and immediately assumed an importance which it could never have attained as a mere dependency. Acting under the advice of the British minister, the Prince Regent threw open the ports of the colony to the ships of all nations friendly to Portugal, gave his sanction to a variety of reforms beneficial to commerce and industry, and even permitted a printing press to be set up, though only for official purposes. From all these benevolent activities Brazil derived great advantages. On the other hand, the Prince Regent's aversion to popular education or anything that might savor of democracy and the greed of his followers for place and distinction alienated his colonial subjects. They could not fail to contrast autocracy in Brazil with the liberal ideas that had made headway elsewhere in Spanish America. As a consequence a spirit of unrest arose which boded ill for the maintenance of Portuguese rule.

CHAPTER III

"INDEPENDENCE OR DEATH"

THE restoration of Ferdinand VII to his throne in 1814 encouraged the liberals of Spain, no less than the loyalists of Spanish America, to hope that the "old King" would now grant a new dispensation. Freedom of commerce and a fair measure of popular representation in government, it was believed, would compensate both the mother country for the suffering which it had undergone during the Peninsular War and the colonies for the trials to which loyalty had been subjected. But Ferdinand VII was a typical Bourbon. Nothing less than an absolute reestablishment of the earlier régime would satisfy him. On both sides of the Atlantic, therefore, the liberals were forced into opposition to the crown, although they were so far apart that they could not coöperate with each other. Independence was to be the fortune of the Spanish Americans, and a continuance of despotism, for a while, the lot of the Spaniards.

As the region of the viceroyalty of La Plata had been the first to cast off the authority of the home government, so it was the first to complete its separation from Spain. Despite the fact that disorder was rampant everywhere and that most of the local districts could not or would not send deputies, a congress that assembled at Tucumán voted on July 9, 1816, to declare the "United Provinces in South America" independent. Comprehensive though the expression was, it applied only to the central part of the former viceroyalty, and even there it was little more than an aspiration. Mistrust of the authorities at Buenos Aires, insistence upon provincial autonomy, failure to agree upon a particular kind of republican government, and a lingering inclination to monarchy made progress toward national unity impossible. In 1819, to be sure, a constitution was adopted, providing for a centralized government, but in the country at large it encountered too much resistance from those who favored a federal government to become effective.

In the Banda Oriental, over most of which Artigas and his horsemen held sway, chaotic conditions invited aggression from the direction of Brazil. This East Bank of the Uruguay had long been disputed territory between Spain and Portugal; and now its definite acquisition by the latter seemed an easy undertaking. Instead, however, the task turned out to be a truly formidable one. Montevideo, feebly defended by the forces of the Government at Buenos Aires, soon capitulated, but four years elapsed before the rest of the country could be subdued. Artigas fled to Paraguay, where he fell into the clutches of Francia, never to escape. In 1821 the Banda Oriental was annexed to Brazil as the Cisplatine Province.

Over Paraguay that grim and somber potentate, known as "The Supreme One" — *El Supremo* — presided with iron hand. In 1817 Francia set up a despotism unique in the annals of South America. Fearful lest contact with the outer world might weaken his tenacious grip upon his subjects, whom he terrorized into obedience, he barred approach to the country and suffered no one to leave it. He organized and drilled an army obedient to his will. When he went forth by day, attended by an escort of cavalry, the doors and windows of houses had to be kept closed and no one was allowed on the streets. Night he spent till a late hour in reading and study, changing his bedroom frequently to avoid assassination. Religious functions that might disturb the public peace he forbade. Compelling the bishop of Asunción to resign on account of senile debility, Francia himself assumed the episcopal office. Even intermarriage among the old colonial families he prohibited, so as to reduce all to a common social level. He attained his object. Paraguay became a quiet state, whatever might be said of its neighbors!

Elsewhere in southern Spanish America a brilliant feat of arms brought to the fore its most distinguished soldier. This was José de San Martín of La Plata. Like Miranda, he had been an officer in the Spanish army and had returned to his native land an ardent apostle of independence. Quick to realize the fact that, so long as Chile remained under royalist control, the possibility of an attack from that quarter was a constant menace to the safety of the newly constituted republic, he conceived the bold plan of organizing near the western frontier an army — composed partly of Chilean refugees and partly of his own countrymen — with which he proposed to cross the Andes and meet the enemy on his own ground. Among these fugitives was the able and valiant

Bernardo O'Higgins, son of an Irish officer who had been viceroy of Peru. Coöperating with O'Higgins, San Martín fixed his headquarters at Mendoza and began to gather and train the four thousand men whom he judged needful for the enterprise.

By January, 1817, the "Army of the Andes" was ready. To cross the mountains meant to transport men, horses, artillery, and stores to an altitude of thirteen thousand feet, where the Uspallata Pass afforded an outlet to Chilean soil. This pass was nearly a mile higher than the Great St. Bernard in the Alps, the crossing of which gave Napoleon Bonaparte such renown. On the 12th of February the hosts of San Martín hurled themselves upon the royalists entrenched on the slopes of Chacabuco and routed them utterly. The battle proved decisive not of the fortunes of Chile alone but of those of all Spanish South America. As a viceroy of Peru later confessed, "it marked the moment when the cause of Spain in the Indies began to recede."

Named supreme director by the people of Santiago, O'Higgins fought vigorously though ineffectually to drive out the royalists who, reinforced from Peru, held the region south of the capital.

That he failed did not deter him from having a vote taken under military auspices, on the strength of which, on February 12, 1818, he declared Chile an independent nation, the date of the proclamation being changed to the 1st of January, so as to make the inauguration of the new era coincident with the entry of the new year. San Martín, meanwhile, had been collecting reinforcements with which to strike the final blow. On the 5th of April, the Battle of Maipo gave him the victory he desired. Except for a few isolated points to the southward, the power of Spain had fallen.

Until the fall of Napoleon in 1815 it had been the native loyalists who had supported the cause of the mother country in the Spanish dominions. Henceforth, free from the menace of the European dictator, Spain could look to her affairs in America, and during the next three years dispatched twenty-five thousand men to bring the colonies to obedience. These soldiers began their task in the northern part of South America, and there they ended it — in failure. To this failure the defection of native royalists contributed, for they were alienated not so much by the presence of the Spanish troops as by the often merciless severity that marked their conduct. The atrocities may have been provoked by the behavior of their opponents; but, be this as it may, the patriots gained recruits after each victory.

A Spanish army of more than ten thousand, under the command of Pablo Morillo, arrived in Venezuela in April, 1815. He found the province relatively tranquil and even disposed to welcome the full restoration of royal government. Leaving a garrison sufficient for the purpose of military occupation, Morillo sailed for Cartagena, the key to New Granada. Besieged by land and sea, the inhabitants of the town maintained for upwards of three months a resistance which, in its heroism, privation, and sacrifice, recalled the memorable defense of Saragossa in the mother country against the French seven years before. With Cartagena taken, regulars and loyalists united to stamp out the rebellion elsewhere. At Bogotá, in particular, the new Spanish viceroy installed by Morillo waged a savage war on all suspected of aiding the patriot cause. He did not spare even women, and one of his victims was a young heroine, Policarpa Salavarrieta by name. Though for her execution three thousand soldiers were detailed, the girl was unterrified by her doom and was earnestly beseeching the loyalists among them to turn their arms against the enemies of their country when a volley stretched her lifeless on the ground.

Meanwhile Bolívar had been fitting out, in Haiti and in the Dutch island of Curaçao, an expedition to take up anew the work of freeing Venezuela. Hardly had the Liberator landed in May, 1816, when dissensions with his fellow officers frustrated any prospect of success. Indeed they obliged him to seek refuge once more in Haiti. Eventually, however, most of the patriot leaders became convinced that, if they were to entertain a hope of success, they must entrust their fortunes to Bolívar as supreme commander. Their chances of success were increased furthermore by the support of the *llaneros* who had been won over to the cause of independence. Under their redoubtable chieftain, José Antonio Páez, these fierce and ruthless horsemen performed many a feat of valor in the campaigns which followed.

Once again on Venezuelan soil, Bolívar determined to transfer his operations to the eastern part of the country, which seemed to offer better strategic advantages than the region about Caracas. But even here the jealousy of his officers, the insubordination of the free lances, the stubborn resistance of the loyalists — upheld by the wealthy and conservative classes and the able generalship of Morillo, who had returned from New Granada — made the situation of the Liberator all through 1817 and 1818 extremely precarious. Happily for his fading fortunes, his hands were strengthened from abroad. The United States had recognized the belligerency of several of the revolutionary governments in South America and had sent diplomatic agents to them. Great Britain had blocked every attempt of Ferdinand VII to obtain help from the Holy Alliance in reconquering his dominions. And Ferdinand had contributed to his own undoing by failing to heed the urgent requests of Morillo for reinforcements to fill his dwindling ranks. More decisive still were the services of some five thousand British, Irish, French, and German volunteers, who were often the mainstay of Bolívar and his lieutenants during the later phases of the struggle, both in Venezuela and elsewhere.

For some time the Liberator had been evolving a plan of attack upon the royalists in New Granada, similar to the offensive campaign which San Martín had conducted in Chile. More than that, he had conceived the idea, once independence had been attained, of uniting the western part of the viceroyalty with Venezuela into a single republic. The latter plan he laid down before a Congress which assembled at Angostura in February, 1819, and which promptly chose him President of the republic and vested him with the powers of dictator. In June, at the head of 2100 men, he started on his perilous journey over the Andes.

Up through the passes and across bleak plateaus the little army struggled till it reached the banks of the rivulet of Boyacá, in the very heart of New Granada. Here, on the 7th of August, Bolívar inflicted on the royalist forces a tremendous defeat that gave the deathblow to the domination of Spain in northern South America. On his triumphal return to Angostura, the Congress signalized the victory by declaring the whole of the viceroyalty an independent state under the name of the "Republic of Colombia" and chose the Liberator as its provisional President. Two years later, a fundamental law it had adopted was ratified with certain changes by another Congress assembled at Rosario de Cúcuta, and Bolívar was made permanent President.

Southward of Colombia lay the viceroyalty of Peru, the oldest, richest, and most conservative of the larger Spanish dominions on the continent. Intact, except for the loss of Chile, it had found territorial compensation by stretching its power over the provinces of Quito and Charcas, the one wrenched off from the former New Granada, the other torn away from what had been La Plata. Predominantly royalist in sentiment, it was like a huge wedge thrust in between the two independent areas. By thus cutting off the patriots of the north from their comrades in the south, it threatened both with destruction of their liberty.

Again fortune intervened from abroad, this time directly from Spain itself. Ferdinand VII, who had gathered an army of twenty thousand men at Cadiz, was ready to deliver a crushing blow at the colonies when in January, 1820, a mutiny among the troops and revolution throughout the country entirely frustrated the plan. But although that reactionary monarch was compelled to accept the Constitution of 1812, the Spanish liberals were unwilling to concede to their fellows in America anything more substantial than representation in the Cortes. Independence they would not tolerate. On the other hand, the example of the mother country in arms against its King in the name of liberty could not fail to give heart to the cause of liberation in the provinces oversea and to hasten its achievement.

The first important efforts to profit by this situation were made by the patriots in Chile. Both San Martín and O'Higgins had perceived that the only effective way to eliminate the Peruvian wedge was to gain control of its approaches by sea. The Chileans had already won some success in this direction when the fiery and imperious Scotch sailor, Thomas Cochrane, Earl of Dundonald, appeared on the scene and offered to organize a navy. At length a squadron was put under his command. With upwards of four thousand troops in charge of San Martín the expedition set sail for Peru late in August, 1820.

While Cochrane busied himself in destroying the Spanish blockade, his comrade in arms marched up to the very gates of Lima, the capital, and everywhere aroused enthusiasm for emancipation. When negotiations, which had been begun by the viceroy and continued by a special commissioner from Spain, failed to swerve the patriot leader from his demand for a recognition of independence, the royalists decided to evacuate the town and to withdraw into the mountainous region of the interior. San Martín, thereupon, entered the capital at the head of his army of liberation and summoned the inhabitants to a town meeting at which they might determine for themselves what action should be taken. The result was easily foreseen. On July 28, 1821, Peru was declared independent, and a few days later San Martín was invested with supreme command under the title of "Protector."

But the triumph of the new Protector did not last long. For some reason he failed to understand that the withdrawal of the royalists from the neighborhood of the coast was merely a strategic retreat that made the occupation of the capital a more or less empty performance. This blunder and a variety of other mishaps proved destined to blight his military career. Unfortunate in the choice of his subordinates and unable to retain their confidence; accused of irresolution and even of cowardice; abandoned by Cochrane, who sailed off to Chile and left the army stranded; incapable of restraining his soldiers from indulgence in the pleasures of Lima; now severe, now lax in an administration that alienated the sympathies of the influential class, San Martín was indeed an unhappy figure. It soon became clear that he must abandon all hope of ever conquering the citadel of

Spanish power in South America unless
prevail upon Bolívar to help him.

A junction of the forces of the two great leaders was perfectly feasible, after the last important foothold of the Spaniards on the coast of Venezuela had been broken by the Battle of Carabobo, on July 24, 1821. Whether such a union would be made, however, depended upon two things: the ultimate disposition of the province of Quito, lying between Colombia and Peru, and the attitude which Bolívar and San Martín themselves should assume toward each other. A revolution of the previous year at the seaport town of Guayaquil in that province had installed an independent government which besought the Liberator to sustain its existence. Prompt to avail himself of so auspicious an opportunity of uniting this former division of the viceroyalty of New Granada to his republic of Colombia, Bolívar appointed Antonio José de Sucre, his ablest lieutenant and probably the most efficient of all Spanish American soldiers of the time, to assume charge of the campaign. On his arrival at Guayaquil, this officer found the inhabitants at odds among themselves. Some, hearkening to the pleas of an agent of San Martín, favored union with Peru; others, yielding to the arguments of a representative of Bolívar, urged annexation to Colombia; still others regarded absolute independence as most desirable. Under these circumstances Sucre for a while made little headway against the royalists concentrated in the mountainous parts of the country, despite the partial support he received from troops which were sent by the southern commander. At length, on May 24, 1822, scaling the flanks of the volcano of Pichincha, near the capital town of Quito itself, he delivered the blow for freedom. Here Bolívar, who had fought his way overland amid tremendous difficulties, joined him and started for Guayaquil, where he and San Martín were to hold their memorable interview.

No characters in Spanish American history have called forth so much controversy about their respective merits and demerits as these two heroes of independence — Bolívar and San Martín. Even now it seems quite impossible to obtain from the admirers of either an opinion that does full justice to both; and foreigners who venture to pass judgment are almost certain to provoke criticism from one set of partisans or the other. Both Bolívar and San Martín were sons of country gentlemen, aristocratic by lineage and devoted to the cause of independence. Bolívar was alert, dauntless, brilliant, impetuous, vehemently patriotic, and yet often capricious, domineering, vain, ostentatious, and disdainful of moral considerations — a masterful man, fertile in intellect, fluent in speech and with pen, an inspiring leader and one born to command in state and army. Quite as earnest, equally courageous, and upholding in private life a higher standard of morals, San Martín was relatively calm, cautious, almost taciturn in manner, and slower in thought and action. He was primarily a soldier, fitted to organize and conduct expeditions, rather than a man endowed with that supreme confidence in himself which brings enthusiasm, affection, and loyalty in its train.

When San Martín arrived at Guayaquil, late in July, 1822, his hope of annexing the province of Quito to Peru was rudely shattered by the news that Bolívar had already declared it a part of Colombia. Though it was outwardly cordial and even effusive, the meeting of the two men held out no prospect of accord. In an interchange of views which lasted but a few hours, mutual suspicion, jealousy, and resentment prevented their reaching an effective understanding. The Protector, it would seem, thought the Liberator actuated by a boundless ambition that would not endure resistance.

Bolívar fancied San Martín a crafty schemer plotting for his own advancement. They failed to agree on the three fundamental points essential to their further coöperation. Bolívar declined to give up the province of Quito. He refused also to send an army into Peru unless he could command it in person, and then he declined to undertake the expedition on the ground that as President of Colombia he ought not to leave the territory of the republic. Divining this pretext, San Martín offered to serve under his orders — a feint that Bolívar parried by protesting that he would not hear of any such self-denial on the part of a brother officer.

Above all, the two men differed about the political form to be adopted for the new independent states. Both of them realized that anything like genuine democracies was quite impossible of attainment for many years to come, and that strong administrations would be needful to tide the Spanish Americans over from the political inexperience of colonial days and the disorders of revolution to intelligent self-government, which could come only after a practical acquaintance with public concerns on a large scale. San Martín believed that a limited monarchy was the best form of government under the circumstances. Bolívar held fast to the idea of a centralized or unitary republic, in which actual power should be exercised by a life president and an hereditary senate until the people, represented in a lower house, should have gained a sufficient amount of political experience.

When San Martín returned to Lima he found affairs in a worse state than ever. The tyrannical conduct of the officer he had left in charge had provoked an uprising that made his position insupportable. Conscious that his mission had come to an end and certain that, unless he gave way, a collision with Bolívar was inevitable, San Martín resolved to sacrifice himself lest harm befall the common cause in which both had done such yeoman service. Accordingly he resigned his power into the hands of a constituent congress and left the country. But when he found that no happier fortune awaited him in Chile and in his own native land, San Martín decided to abandon Spanish America forever and go into self-imposed exile. Broken in health and spirit, he took up his residence in France, a recipient of bounty from a Spaniard who had once been his comrade in arms.

Meanwhile in the Mexican part of the viceroyalty of New Spain the cry of independence raised by Morelos and his bands of Indian followers had been stifled by the capture and execution of the leader. But the cause of independence was not dead even if its achievement was to be entrusted to other hands. Eager to emulate the example of their brethren in South America, small parties of Spaniards and Creoles fought to overturn the despotic rule of Ferdinand VII, only to encounter defeat from the royalists. Then came the Revolution of 1820 in the mother country. Forthwith demands were heard for a recognition of the liberal régime. Fearful of being displaced from power, the viceroy with the support of the clergy and aristocracy ordered Agustín de Iturbide, a Creole officer who had been an active royalist, to quell an insurrection in the southern part of the country.

The choice of this soldier was unfortunate. Personally ambitious and cherishing in secret the thought of independence, Iturbide, faithless to his trust, entered into negotiations with the insurgents which culminated February 24, 1821, in what was called the "Plan of Iguala." It contained three main provisions, or "guarantees," as they were termed: the maintenance of the Catholic religion to the exclusion of all others; the establishment of a constitutional monarchy separate from Spain and ruled by Ferdinand himself, or, if he declined the honor, by some other European prince; and the union of Mexicans and Spaniards without distinction of caste or privilege. A temporary government also, in the form of a junta presided over by the viceroy, was to be created; and provision was made for the organization of an "Army of the Three Guarantees."

Despite opposition from the royalists, the plan won increasing favor. Powerless to thwart it and inclined besides to a policy of conciliation, the new viceroy, Juan O'Donojú, agreed to ratify it on condition — in obedience to a suggestion from Iturbide — that the parties concerned should be at liberty, if they desired, to choose any one as emperor, whether he were of a reigning family or not. Thereupon, on the 28th of September, the provisional Government installed at the city of Mexico announced the consummation of an "enterprise rendered eternally memorable, which a genius beyond all admiration and eulogy, love and glory of his country, began at Iguala, prosecuted and carried into effect, overcoming obstacles almost insuperable" — and declared the independence of the "Mexican Empire." The act was followed by the appointment of a regency to govern until the accession of Ferdinand VII, or some other personage, to the imperial throne. Of this body Iturbide assumed the presidency, which carried with it the powers of commander in chief and a salary of 120,000 *pesos*, paid from the day on which the Plan of Iguala was signed. O'Donojú contented himself with membership on the board and a salary of one-twelfth that amount, until his speedy demise removed from the scene the last of the Spanish viceroys in North America.

One step more was needed. Learning that the Cortes in Spain had rejected the entire scheme, Iturbide allowed his soldiers to acclaim him emperor, and an unwilling Congress saw itself obliged to ratify the choice. On July 21, 1822, the destinies of the country were committed to the charge of Agustín the First.

As in the area of Mexico proper, so in the Central American part of the viceroyalty of New Spain, the Spanish Revolution of 1820 had unexpected results. Here in the five little provinces composing the captaincy general of Guatemala there was much unrest, but nothing of a serious nature occurred until after news had been brought of the Plan of Iguala and its immediate outcome. Thereupon a popular assembly met at the capital town of

Guatemala, and on September 15, 1821, declared the country an independent state. This radical act accomplished, the patriot leaders were unable to proceed further. Demands for the establishment of a federation, for a recognition of local autonomy, for annexation to Mexico, were all heard, and none, except the last, was answered. While the "Imperialists" and "Republicans" were arguing it out, a message from Emperor Agustín announced that he would not allow the new state to remain independent. On submission of the matter to a vote of the *cabildos*, most of them approved reunion with the northern neighbor. Salvador alone among the provinces held out until troops from Mexico overcame its resistance.

On the continents of America, Spain had now lost nearly all its possessions. In 1822 the United States, which had already acquired East Florida on its own account, led off in recognizing the independence of the several republics. Only in Peru and Charcas the royalists still battled on behalf of the mother country. In the West Indies, Santo Domingo followed the lead of its sister colonies on the mainland by asserting in 1821 its independence; but its brief independent life was snuffed out by the negroes of Haiti, once more a republic, who spread their control over the entire island. Cuba also felt the impulse of the times. But, apart from the agitation of secret societies like the "Rays and Suns of Bolívar," which was soon checked, the colony remained tranquil.

In Portuguese America the knowledge of what had occurred throughout the Spanish dominions could not fail to awaken a desire for independence. The Prince Regent was well aware of the discontent of the Brazilians, but he thought to allay it by substantial concessions. In 1815 he proceeded to elevate the colony to substantial equality with the mother country by joining them under the title of "United Kingdom of Portugal, Brazil, and the Algarves." The next year the Prince Regent himself became King under the name of John IV. The flame of discontent, nevertheless, continued to smolder. Republican outbreaks, though quelled without much difficulty, recurred. Even the reforms which had been instituted by John himself while Regent, and which had assured freer communication with the world at large, only emphasized more and more the absurdity of permitting a feeble little land like Portugal to retain its hold upon a region so extensive and valuable as Brazil.

The events of 1820 in Portugal hastened the movement toward independence. Fired by the success of their Spanish comrades, the Portuguese liberals forthwith rose in revolt, demanded the establishment of a limited monarchy, and insisted that the King return to his people. In similar fashion, also, they drew up a constitution which provided for the representation of Brazil by deputies in a future Cortes. Beyond this they would concede no special privileges to the colony. Indeed their idea seems to have been that, with the King once more in Lisbon, their own liberties would be secure and those of Brazil would be reduced to what were befitting a mere dependency. Yielding to the inevitable, the King decided to return to Portugal, leaving the young Crown Prince to act as Regent in the colony. A critical moment for the little country and its big dominion oversea had indubitably arrived. John understood the trend of the times, for on the eve of his departure he said to his son: "Pedro, if Brazil is to separate itself from Portugal, as seems likely, you take the crown yourself before any one else gets it!"

Pedro was liberal in sentiment, popular among the Brazilians, and well-disposed toward the aspirations of the country for a larger measure of freedom, and yet not blind to the interests of the dynasty of Braganza. He readily listened to the urgent pleas of the leaders of the separatist party against obeying the repressive mandates of the Cortes. Laws which abolished the central government of the colony and made the various provinces individually subject to Portugal he declined to notice. With equal promptness he refused to heed an order bidding him return to Portugal immediately. To a delegation of prominent Brazilians he said emphatically: "For the good of all and the general welfare of the nation, I shall stay." More than that, in May, 1822, he accepted from the municipality of Rio de Janeiro the title of "Perpetual and Constitutional Defender of Brazil," and in a series of proclamations urged the people of the country to begin the great work of emancipation by forcibly resisting, if needful, any attempt at coercion.

Pedro now believed the moment had come to take the final step. While on a journey through the province of São Paulo, he was overtaken on the 7th of September, near a little stream called the Ypiranga, by messengers with dispatches from Portugal. Finding that the Cortes had annulled his acts and declared his ministers guilty of treason, Pedro forthwith proclaimed Brazil an independent state. The "cry of Ypiranga" was echoed with tremendous enthusiasm throughout the country. When Pedro appeared in the theater at Rio de Janeiro, a few days later, wearing on his arm a ribbon on which were inscribed the words "Independence or Death," he was given a tumultuous ovation. On the first day of December the youthful monarch assumed the title of Emperor, and Brazil thereupon took its place among the nations of America.

CHAPTER IV

PLOUGHING THE SEA

WHEN the La Plata Congress at Tucumán took the decisive action that severed the bond with Spain, it uttered a prophecy for all Spanish America. To quote its language: "Vast and fertile regions, climates benign and varied, abundant means of subsistence, treasures of gold and silver . . . and fine productions of every sort will attract to our continent innumerable thousands of immigrants, to whom we shall open a safe place of refuge and extend a beneficent protection." More hopeful still were the words of a spokesman for another independent country: "United, neither the empire of the Assyrians, the Medes or the Persians, the Macedonian or the Roman Empire, can ever be compared with this colossal republic."

Very different was the vision of Bolívar. While a refugee in Jamaica he wrote: "We are a little human species; we possess a world apart . . . new in almost all the arts and sciences, and yet old, after a fashion, in the uses of civil society. . . . Neither Indians nor Europeans, we are a species that lies midway. . . . Is it conceivable that a people recently freed of its chains can launch itself into the sphere of liberty without shattering its wings, like Icarus, and plunging into the abyss? Such a prodigy is inconceivable, never beheld." Toward the close of his career he declared: "The majority are *mestizos*, mulattoes, Indians, and negroes. An ignorant people is a blunt instrument for its own destruction. To it liberty means license, patriotism means disloyalty, and justice means vengeance." "Independence," he exclaimed, "is the only good we have achieved, at the cost of everything else."

Whether the abounding confidence of the prophecy or the anxious doubt of the vision would come true, only the future could tell. In 1822, at all events, optimism was the watchword and the total exclusion of Spain from South America the goal of Bolívar and his lieutenants, as they started southward to complete the work of emancipation which had been begun by San Martín.

The patriots of Peru, indeed, had fallen into straits so desperate that an appeal to the Liberator offered the only hope of salvation. While the royalists under their able and vigilant leader, José Canterac, continued to strengthen their grasp upon the interior of the country and to uphold the power of the viceroy, the President chosen by the Congress had been driven by the enemy from Lima. A number of the legislators in wrath thereupon declared the President deposed. Not to be outdone, that functionary on his part declared the Congress dissolved. The malcontents immediately proceeded to elect a new chief magistrate, thus bringing two Presidents into the field and inaugurating a spectacle destined to become all too common in the subsequent annals of Spanish America.

When Bolívar arrived at Callao, the seaport of Lima, in September, 1823, he acted with prompt vigor. He expelled one President, converted the other into a passive instrument of his will, declined to promulgate a constitution that the Congress had prepared, and, after obtaining from that body an appointment to supreme command, dissolved the Congress without further ado. Unfortunately none of these radical measures had any perceptible effect upon the military situation. Though Bolívar gathered together an army made up of Colombians, Peruvians, and remnants of San Martín's force, many months elapsed before he could venture upon a serious campaign. Then events in Spain played into his hands. The reaction that had followed the restoration of Ferdinand VII to absolute power crossed the ocean and split the royalists into opposing factions. Quick to seize the chance thus afforded, Bolívar marched over the Andes to the plain of Junín. There, on August 6, 1824, he repelled an onslaught by Canterac and drove that leader back in headlong flight. Believing, however, that the position he held was too perilous to risk an offensive, he entrusted the military command to Sucre and returned to headquarters.

The royalists had now come to realize that only a supreme effort could save them. They must overwhelm Sucre before reinforcements could reach him, and to this end an army of upwards of ten thousand was assembled. On the 9th of December it encountered Sucre and his six thousand soldiers in the valley of Ayacucho, or "Corner of Death," where the patriot general had entrenched his army with admirable skill. The result was a total defeat for the royalists — the Waterloo of Spain in South America. The battle thus won by ragged and hungry soldiers — whose countersign the night before had been "bread and cheese" — threw off the yoke of the mother country forever. The viceroy fell wounded into their hands and Canterac surrendered. On receipt of the glorious news, the people of Lima greeted Bolívar with wild enthusiasm. A Congress prolonged his dictatorship amid adulations that bordered on the grotesque.

Eastward of Peru in the vast mountainous region of Charcas, on the very heights of South America, the royalists still found a refuge. In January, 1825, a patriot general at the town of La Paz undertook on his own responsibility to declare the entire province independent, alike of Spain, Peru, and the United Provinces of La Plata. This action was too precipitous, not to say presumptuous, to suit Bolívar and Sucre. The better to control the situation, the former went up to La Paz and the latter to Chuquisaca, the capital, where a Congress was to assemble for the purpose of imparting a more orderly turn to affairs. Under the direction of the "Marshal of Ayacucho," as Sucre was now called, the Congress issued on the 6th of August a formal declaration of independence. In honor of the Liberator it christened the new republic "Bolívar" — later Latinized into "Bolivia" — and conferred upon him the presidency so long as he might choose to remain. In November, 1826, a new Congress which had been summoned to draft a constitution accepted, with slight modifications, an instrument that the Liberator himself had prepared. That body also renamed the capital "Sucre" and chose the hero of Ayacucho as President of the republic.

Now, the Liberator thought, was the opportune moment to impose upon his territorial namesake a constitution embodying his ideas of a stable government which would give Spanish Americans eventually the political experience they needed. Providing for an autocracy represented by a life President, it ran the gamut of aristocracy and democracy, all the way from "censors" for life, who were to watch over the due enforcement of the laws, down to senators and "tribunes" chosen by electors, who in turn were to be named by a select citizenry. Whenever actually present in the territory of the republic, the Liberator was to enjoy supreme command, in case he wished to exercise it.

In 1826 Simón Bolívar stood at the zenith of his glory and power. No adherents of the Spanish régime were left in South America to menace the freedom of its independent states. In January a resistance kept up for nine years by a handful of royalists lodged on the remote island of Chiloé, off the southern coast of Chile, had been broken, and the garrison at the fortress of Callao had laid down its arms after a valiant struggle. Among Spanish Americans no one was comparable to the marvelous man who had founded three great republics stretching from the Caribbean Sea to the Tropic of Capricorn. Hailed as the "Liberator" and the "Terror of Despots," he was also acclaimed by the people as the "Redeemer, the First-Born Son of the New World!" National destinies were committed to his charge, and equestrian statues were erected in his honor. In the popular imagination he was ranked with Napoleon as a peerless conqueror, and with Washington as the father of his country. That megalomania should have seized the mind of the Liberator under circumstances like these is not strange.

Ever a zealous advocate of large states, Bolívar was an equally ardent partisan of confederation. As president of three republics — of Colombia actually, and of its satellites, Peru and Bolivia, through his lieutenants — he could afford now to carry out the plan that he had long since cherished of assembling at the town of Panamá, on Colombian soil, an "august congress" representative of the independent countries of America. Here, on the isthmus created by nature to join the continents, the nations created by men should foregather and proclaim fraternal accord. Presenting to the autocratic governments of Europe a solid front of resistance to their pretensions as well as a visible symbol of unity in sentiment, such a Congress by meeting periodically would also promote friendship among the republics of the western hemisphere and supply a convenient means of settling their disputes.

At this time the United States was regarded by its sister republics with all the affection which gratitude for services rendered to the cause of emancipation could evoke. Was it not itself a republic, its people a democracy, its development astounding, and its future radiant with hope? The pronouncement of President Monroe, in 1823, protesting against interference on the part of European powers with the liberties of independent America, afforded the clearest possible proof that the great northern republic was a natural protector, guide, and friend whose advice and coöperation ought to be invoked. The United States was accordingly asked to take part in the assembly — not to concert military measures, but simply to join its fellows to the southward in a solemn proclamation of the Monroe Doctrine by America at large and to discuss means of suppressing the slave trade.

The Congress that met at Panamá, in June, 1826, afforded scant encouragement to Bolívar's roseate hope of inter-American solidarity. Whether because of the difficulties of travel, or because of internal dissensions, or because of the suspicion that the megalomania of the Liberator had awakened in Spanish America, only the four continental countries nearest the isthmus — Mexico, Central America, Colombia, and Peru — were represented. The delegates, nevertheless, signed a compact of "perpetual union, league, and confederation," provided for mutual assistance to be rendered by the several nations in time of war, and arranged to have the Areopagus of the Americas transferred to Mexico. None of the acts of this Congress was ratified by the republics concerned, except the agreement for union, which was adopted by Colombia.

Disheartening to Bolívar as this spectacle was, it proved to be merely the first of a series of calamities which were to overshadow the later years of the Liberator. His grandiose political structure began to crumble, for it was built on the shifting sands of a fickle popularity. The more he urged a general acceptance of the principles of his autocratic constitution, the surer were his followers that he coveted royal honors. In December he imposed his instrument upon Peru. Then he learned that a meeting in Venezuela, presided over by Páez, had declared itself in favor of separation from Colombia. Hardly had he left Peru to check this movement when an uprising at Lima deposed his representative and led to the summons of a Congress which, in June, 1827, restored the former constitution and chose a new President. In Quito, also, the government of the unstable dictator was overthrown.

Alarmed by symptoms of disaffection which also appeared in the western part of the republic, Bolívar hurried to Bogotá. There in the hope of removing the growing antagonism, he offered his "irrevocable" resignation, as he had done on more than one occasion before. Though the malcontents declined to accept his withdrawal from office, they insisted upon his calling a constitutional convention. Meeting at Ocaña, in April, 1828, that body proceeded to abolish the life tenure of the presidency, to limit the powers of the executive, and to increase those of the legislature. Bolívar managed to quell the opposition in dictatorial fashion; but his prestige had by this time fallen so low that an attempt was made to assassinate him. The severity with which he punished the conspirators served only to diminish still more the popular confidence which he had once enjoyed. Even in Bolivia his star of destiny had set. An outbreak of Colombian troops at the capital forced the faithful Sucre to resign and leave the country. The constitution was then modified to meet the demand for a less autocratic government, and a new chief magistrate was installed.

Desperately the Liberator strove to ward off the impending collapse. Though he recovered possession of the division of Quito, a year of warfare failed to win back Peru, and he was compelled to renounce all pretense of governing it. Feeble in body and distracted in mind, he condemned bitterly the machinations of his enemies. "There is no good faith in Colombia," he exclaimed, "neither among men nor among nations. Treaties are paper; constitutions, books; elections, combats; liberty, anarchy, and life itself a torment."

But the hardest blow was yet to fall. Late in December, 1829, an assembly at Caracas declared Venezuela a separate state. The great republic was rent in twain, and even what was left soon split apart. In May, 1830, came the final crash. The Congress at Bogotá drafted a constitution, providing for a separate republic to bear the old Spanish name of "New Granada," accepted definitely the resignation of Bolívar, and granted him a pension. Venezuela, his native land, set up a congress of its own and demanded that he be exiled. The division of Quito declared itself independent, under the name of the "Republic of the Equator" (Ecuador). Everywhere the artificial handiwork of the Liberator lay in ruins. "America is ungovernable. Those who have served in the revolution have ploughed the sea," was his despairing cry.

Stricken to death, the fallen hero retired to an estate near Santa Marta. Here, like his famous rival, San Martín, in France, he found hospitality at the hands of a Spaniard. On December 17, 1830, the Liberator gave up his troubled soul.

While Bolívar's great republic was falling apart, the United Provinces of La Plata had lost practically all semblance of cohesion. So broad were their notions of liberty that the several provinces maintained a substantial independence of one another, while within each province the *caudillos*, or partisan chieftains, fought among themselves.

Buenos Aires alone managed to preserve a measure of stability. This comparative peace was due to the financial and commercial measures devised by Bernardino Rivadavia, one of the most capable statesmen of the time, and to the energetic manner in which disorder was suppressed by Juan Manuel de Rosas, commander of the *gaucho*, or cowboy, militia. Thanks also to the former leader, the provinces were induced in 1826 to join in framing a constitution of a unitary character, which vested in the administration at Buenos Aires the power of appointing the local governors and of controlling foreign affairs. The name of the country was at the same time changed to that of the "Argentine Confederation" — a Latin rendering of "La Plata."

No sooner had Rivadavia assumed the presidency under the new order of things than dissension at home and warfare abroad threatened to destroy all that he had accomplished. Ignoring the terms of the constitution, the provinces had already begun to reject the supremacy of Buenos Aires, when the outbreak of a struggle with Brazil forced the contending parties for a while to unite in the face of the common enemy. As before, the object of international dispute was the region of the Banda Oriental. The rule of Brazil had not been oppressive, but the people of its Cisplatine Province, attached by language and sympathy to their western neighbors, longed nevertheless to be free of foreign control. In April, 1825, a band of thirty-three refugees arrived from Buenos Aires and started a revolution which spread throughout the country. Organizing a provisional government, the insurgents proclaimed independence of Brazil and incorporation with the United Provinces of La Plata. As soon as the authorities at Buenos Aires had approved this action, war was inevitable. Though the Brazilians were decisively beaten at the Battle of Ituzaingó, on February 20, 1827, the struggle lasted until August 28, 1828, when mediation by Great Britain led to the conclusion of a treaty at Rio de Janeiro, by which both Brazil and the Argentine Confederation recognized the absolute independence of the disputed province as the republic of Uruguay.

Instead of quieting the discord that prevailed among the Argentinos, these victories only fomented trouble. The federalists had ousted Rivadavia and discarded the constitution, but the federal idea for which they stood had several meanings. To an inhabitant of Buenos Aires federalism meant domination by the capital, not only over the province of the same name but over the other provinces; whereas, to the people of the provinces, and even to many of federalist faith in the province of Buenos Aires itself, the term stood for the idea of a loose confederation in which each provincial governor or chieftain should be practically supreme in his own district, so long as he could maintain himself. The Unitaries were opponents of both, except in so far as their insistence upon a centralized form of government for the nation would necessarily lead to the location of that government at Buenos Aires. This peculiar dual contest between the town and the province of Buenos Aires, and of the other provinces against either or both, persisted for the next sixty years. In 1829, however, a prolonged lull set in, when Rosas, the *gaucho* leader, having won in company with other *caudillos* a decisive triumph over the Unitaries, entered the capital and took supreme command.

In Chile the course of events had assumed quite a different aspect. Here, in 1818, a species of constitution had been adopted by popular vote in a manner that appeared to show remarkable unanimity, for the books in which the "ayes" and "noes" were to be recorded contained no entries in the negative! What the records really prove is that O'Higgins, the Supreme Director, enjoyed the confidence of the ruling class. In exercise of the autocratic power entrusted to him, he now proceeded to introduce a variety of administrative reforms of signal advantage to the moral and material welfare of the country. But as the danger of conquest from any quarter lessened, the demand for a more democratic organization grew louder, until in 1822 it became so persistent that O'Higgins called a convention to draft a new fundamental law. But its provisions suited neither himself nor his opponents. Thereupon, realizing that his views of the political capacity of the people resembled those of Bolívar and were no longer applicable, and that his reforms had aroused too much hostility, the Supreme Director resigned his post and retired to Peru. Thus another hero of emancipation had met the ingratitude for which republics are notorious.

Political convulsions in the country followed the abdication of O'Higgins. Not only had the spirit of the strife between Unitaries and Federalists been communicated to Chile from the neighboring republic to the eastward, but two other parties or factions, divided on still different lines, had arisen. These were the Conservative and the Liberal, or

Bigwigs (*pelucones*) and Greenhorns (*pipiolos*), as the adherents of the one derisively dubbed the partisans of the other. Although in the ups and downs of the struggle two constitutions were adopted, neither sufficed to quiet the agitation. Not until 1830, when the Liberals sustained an utter defeat on the field of battle, did the country enter upon a period of quiet progress along conservative lines. From that time onward it presented a surprising contrast to its fellow republics, which were beset with afflictions.

Far to the northward, the Empire of Mexico set up by Iturbide in 1822 was doomed to a speedy fall. "Emperor by divine providence," that ambitious adventurer inscribed on his coins, but his countrymen knew that the bayonets of his soldiers were the actual mainstay of his pretentious title. Neither his earlier career nor the size of his following was sufficiently impressive to assure him popular support if the military prop gave way. His lavish expenditures, furthermore, and his arbitrary replacement of the Congress by a docile body which would authorize forced loans at his command, steadily undermined his position. Apart from the faults of Iturbide himself, the popular sentiment of a country bordering immediately upon the United States could not fail to be colored by the ideas and institutions of its great neighbor. So, too, the example of what had been accomplished, in form at least, by their kinsmen elsewhere in America was bound to wield a potent influence on the minds of the Mexicans. As a result, their desire for a republic grew stronger from day to day.

Iturbide, in fact, had not enjoyed his exalted rank five months when Antonio López de Santa Anna, a young officer destined later to become a conspicuous figure in Mexican history, started a revolt to replace the "Empire" by a republic. Though he failed in his object, two of Iturbide's generals joined the insurgents in demanding a restoration of the Congress — an act which, as the hapless "Emperor" perceived, would amount to his dethronement. Realizing his impotence, Iturbide summoned the Congress and announced his abdication. But instead of recognizing this procedure, that body declared his accession itself null and void; it agreed, however, to grant him a pension if he would leave the country and reside in Italy. With this disposition of his person Iturbide complied; but he soon wearied of exile and persuaded himself that he would not lack supporters if he tried to regain his former control in Mexico. This venture he decided to make in complete ignorance of a decree ordering his summary execution if he dared to set foot again on Mexican soil. He had hardly landed in July, 1824, when he was seized and shot.

Since a constituent assembly had declared itself in favor of establishing a federal form of republic patterned after that of the United States, the promulgation of a constitution followed on October 4, 1824, and Guadalupe Victoria, one of the leaders in the revolt against Iturbide, was chosen President of the United Mexican States. Though considerable unrest prevailed toward the close of his term, the new President managed to retain his office for the allotted four years. In most respects, however, the new order of things opened auspiciously. In November, 1825, the surrender of the fortress of San Juan de Ulúa, in the harbor of Vera Cruz, banished the last remnant of Spanish power, and two years later the suppression of plots for the restoration of Ferdinand VII, coupled with the expulsion of a large number of Spaniards, helped to restore calm. There were those even who dared to hope that the federal system would operate as smoothly in Mexico as it had done in the United States.

But the political organization of a country so different from its northern neighbor in population, traditions, and practices, could not rest merely on a basis of imitation, even more or less modified. The artificiality of the fabric became apparent enough as soon as ambitious individuals and groups of malcontents concerted measures to mold it into a likeness of reality. Two main political factions soon appeared. For the form they assumed British and American influences were responsible. Adopting a kind of Masonic organization, the Conservatives and Centralists called themselves *Escoceses* (Scottish-Rite Men), whereas the Radicals and Federalists took the name of *Yorkinos* (York-Rite Men). Whatever their respective slogans and professions of political faith, they were little more than personal followers of rival generals or politicians who yearned to occupy the presidential chair.

Upon the downfall of Iturbide, the malcontents in Central America bestirred themselves to throw off the Mexican yoke. On July 1, 1823, a Congress declared the region an independent republic under the name of the "United Provinces of Central America." In November of the next year, following the precedent established in Mexico, and obedient also to local demand, the new republic issued a constitution, in accordance with which the five little divisions of Guatemala, Honduras, Salvador, Nicaragua, and Costa Rica were to become states of a federal union, each having the privilege of choosing its own local authorities. Immediately Federalists and Centralists, Radicals and Conservatives, all wished, it would seem, to impose their particular viewpoint upon their fellows. The situation was not unlike that in the Argentine Confederation. The efforts of Guatemala — the province in which power had been concentrated under the colonial régime — to assert supremacy over its fellow states, and their refusal to respect either the federal bond or one another's rights made civil war inevitable. The struggle which broke out among Guatemala, Salvador, and Honduras, lasted until 1829, when Francisco Morazán, at the head of the "Allied Army, Upholder of the Law," entered the capital of the republic and assumed dictatorial power.

Of all the Hispanic nations, however, Brazil was easily the most stable. Here the leaders, while clinging to independence, strove to avoid dangerous innovations in government. Rather than create a political system for which the country was not prepared, they established a constitutional monarchy. But Brazil itself was too vast and its interior too difficult of access to allow it to become all at once a unit, either in organization or in spirit. The idea of national solidarity had as yet made scant progress. The old rivalry which existed between the provinces of the north, dominated by Bahia or Pernambuco, and those of the south, controlled by Rio de Janeiro or São Paulo, still made itself felt. What the Empire amounted to, therefore, was an agglomeration of provinces, held together by the personal prestige of a young monarch.

Since the mother country still held parts of northern Brazil, the Emperor entrusted the energetic Cochrane, who had performed such valiant service for Chile and Peru, with the task of expelling the foreign soldiery. When this had been accomplished and a republican outbreak in the same region had been suppressed, the more difficult task of satisfying all parties by a constitution had to be undertaken. There were partisans of monarchy and advocates of republicanism, men of conservative and of liberal sympathies; disagreements, also, between the Brazilians and the native Portuguese residents were frequent. So far as possible

Pedro desired to meet popular desires, and yet without imposing too many limitations on the monarchy itself. But in the assembly called to draft the constitution the liberal members made a determined effort to introduce republican forms. Pedro thereupon dissolved that body and in 1826 promulgated a constitution of his own.

The popularity of the Emperor thereafter soon began to wane, partly because of the scandalous character of his private life, and partly because he declined to observe constitutional restrictions and chose his ministers at will. His insistent war in Portugal to uphold the claims of his daughter to the throne betrayed, or seemed to betray, dynastic ambitions. His inability to hold Uruguay as a Brazilian province, and his continued retention of foreign soldiers who had been employed in the struggle with the Argentine Confederation, for the apparent purpose of quelling possible insurrections in the future, bred much discontent. So also did the restraints he laid upon the press, which had been infected by the liberal movements in neighboring republics. When he failed to subdue these outbreaks, his rule became all the more discredited. Thereupon, menaced by a dangerous uprising at Rio de Janeiro in 1831, he abdicated the throne in favor of his son, Pedro, then five years of age, and set sail for Portugal.

Under the influence of Great Britain the small European mother country had in 1825 recognized the independence of its big transatlantic dominion; but it was not until 1836 that the Cortes of Spain authorized the Crown to enter upon negotiations looking to the same action in regard to the eleven republics which had sprung out of its colonial domain. Even then many years elapsed before the mother country acknowledged the independence of them all.

CHAPTER V

THE AGE OF THE DICTATORS

INDEPENDENCE without liberty and statehood without respect for law are phrases which sum up the situation in Spanish America after the failure of Bolívar's "great design." The outcome was a collection of crude republics, racked by internal dissension and torn by mutual jealousy — *patrias bobas*, or "foolish fatherlands," as one of their own writers has termed them.

Now that the bond of unity once supplied by Spain had been broken, the entire region which had been its continental domain in America dissolved awhile into its elements. The Spanish language, the traditions and customs of the dominant class, and a "republican" form of government, were practically the sole ties which remained. Laws, to be sure, had been enacted, providing for the immediate or gradual abolition of negro slavery and for an improvement in the status of the Indian and half-caste; but the bulk of the inhabitants, as in colonial times, remained outside of the body politic and social. Though the so-called "constitutions" might confer upon the colored inhabitants all the privileges and immunities of citizens if they could read and write, and even a chance to hold office if they could show possession of a sufficient income or of a professional title of some sort, their usual inability to do either made their privileges illusory. Their only share in public concerns lay in performing military service at the behest of their superiors. Even where the language of the constitutions did not exclude the colored inhabitants directly or indirectly, practical authority was exercised by dictators who played the autocrat, or by "liberators" who aimed at the enjoyment of that function themselves.

Not all the dictators, however, were selfish tyrants, nor all the liberators mere pretenders. Disturbed conditions bred by twenty years of warfare, antique methods of industry, a backward commerce, inadequate means of communication, and a population ignorant, superstitious, and scant, made a strong ruler more or less indispensable. Whatever his official designation, the dictator was the logical successor of the Spanish viceroy or captain general, but without the sense of responsibility or the legal restraint of either. These circumstances account for that curious political phase in the development of the Spanish American nations — the presidential despotism.

On the other hand, the men who denounced oppression, unscrupulousness, and venality, and who in rhetorical *pronunciamentos* urged the "people" to overthrow the dictators, were often actuated by motives of patriotism, even though they based their declarations on assumptions and assertions, rather than on principles and facts. Not infrequently a liberator of this sort became "provisional president" until he himself, or some person of his choice, could be elected "constitutional president" — two other institutions more or less peculiar to Spanish America.

In an atmosphere of political theorizing mingled with ambition for personal advancement, both leaders and followers were professed devotees of constitutions. No people, it was thought, could maintain a real republic and be a true democracy if they did not possess a written constitution. The longer this was, and the more precise its definition of powers and liberties, the more authentic the republic and the more genuine the democracy was thought to be. In some countries the notion was carried still farther by an insistence upon frequent changes in the fundamental law or in the actual form of government, not so much to meet imperative needs as to satisfy a zest for experimentation or to suit the whims of mercurial temperaments. The congresses, constituent assemblies, and the like, which drew these instruments, were supposed to be faithful reproductions of similar bodies abroad and to represent the popular will. In fact, however, they were substantially colonial *cabildos*, enlarged into the semblance of a legislature, intent upon local or personal concerns, and lacking any national consciousness. In any case the members were apt to be creatures of a republican despot or else delegates of politicians or petty factions.

Assuming that the leaders had a fairly clear conception of what they wanted, even if the mass of their adherents did not, it is possible to aline the factions or parties somewhat as follows: on the one hand, the unitary, the military, the clerical, the conservative, and the moderate; on the other, the federalist, the civilian, the lay, the liberal, and the radical. Interspersed among them were the advocates of a presidential or congressional system like that of the United States, the upholders of a parliamentary régime like that of European nations, and the supporters of methods of government of a more experimental kind. Broadly speaking, the line of cleavage was made by opinions concerning the form of government and by convictions regarding the relations of Church and State. These opinions were mainly a product of revolutionary experience; these convictions, on the other hand, were a bequest from colonial times.

The Unitaries wished to have a system of government modeled upon that of France. They wanted the various provinces made into administrative districts over which the national authority should exercise full sway. Their direct opponents, the Federalists, resembled to some extent the Antifederalists rather than the party bearing the former title in the earlier history of the United States; but even here an exact analogy fails. They did not seek to have the provinces enjoy local self-government or to have perpetuated the traditions of a sort of municipal home rule handed down from the colonial *cabildos*, so much as to secure the recognition of a number of isolated villages or small towns as sovereign states — which meant turning them over as fiefs to their local chieftains. Federalism, therefore, was the Spanish American expression for a feudalism upheld by military lordlets and their retainers.

Among the measures of reform introduced by one republic or another during the revolutionary period, abolition of the Inquisition had been one of the foremost; otherwise comparatively little was done to curb the influence of the Church. Indeed the earlier constitutions regularly contained articles declaring Roman Catholicism the sole legal faith as well as the religion of the state, and safeguarding in other respects its prestige in the community. Here was an institution, wealthy, proud, and influential, which declined to yield its ancient prerogatives and privileges and to that end relied upon the support of clericals and conservatives who disliked innovations of a democratic sort and viewed askance the entry of immigrants professing an alien faith. Opposed to the Church stood governments verging on bankruptcy, desirous of exercising supreme control, and dominated by individuals eager to put theories of democracy into practice and to throw open the doors of the republic freely to newcomers from other lands. In the opinion of these radicals the Church ought to be deprived both of its property and of its monopoly of education. The one should be turned over to the nation, to which it properly belonged, and should be converted into public utilities; the other should be made absolutely secular, in order to destroy clerical influence over the youthful mind. In this program radicals and liberals concurred with varying degrees of intensity, while the moderates strove to hold the balance between them and their opponents.

Out of this complex situation civil commotions were bound to arise. Occasionally these were real wars, but as a rule only skirmishes or sporadic insurrections occurred. They were called "revolutions," not because some great principle was actually at stake but because the term had been popular ever since the struggle with Spain. As a designation for movements aimed at securing rotation in office, and hence control of the treasury, it was appropriate enough! At all events, whether serious or farcical, the commotions often involved an expenditure in life and money far beyond the value of the interests affected. Further, both the prevalent disorder and the centralization of authority impelled the educated and well-to-do classes to take up their residence at the seat of government. Not a few of the uprisings were, in fact, protests on the part of the neglected folk in the interior of the country against concentration of population, wealth, intellect, and power in the Spanish American capitals.

Among the towns of this sort was Buenos Aires. Here, in 1829, Rosas inaugurated a career of rulership over the Argentine Confederation, culminating in a despotism that made him the most extraordinary figure of his time. Originally a stock-farmer and skilled in all the exercises of the cowboy, he developed an unusual talent for administration. His keen intelligence, supple statecraft, inflexibility of purpose, and vigor of action, united to a shrewd understanding of human follies and passions, gave to his personality a dominance that awed and to his word of command a power that humbled. Over his fellow chieftains who held the provinces in terrorized subjection, he won an ascendancy that insured compliance with his will. The instincts of the multitude he flattered by his generous simplicity, while he enlisted the support of the responsible class by maintaining order in the countryside. The desire, also, of Buenos Aires to be paramount over the other provinces had no small share in strengthening his power.

Relatively honest in money matters, and a stickler for precision and uniformity, Rosas sought to govern a nation in the rough-and-ready fashion of the stock farm. A creature of his environment, no better and no worse than his associates, but only more capable than they, and absolutely convinced that pitiless autocracy was the sole means of creating a nation out of chaotic fragments, this "Robespierre of South America" carried on his despotic sway, regardless of the fury of opponents and the menace of foreign intervention.

During the first three years of his control, however, except for the rigorous suppression of unitary movements and the muzzling of the press, few signs appeared of the "black night of Argentine history" which was soon to close down on the land. Realizing that the auspicious moment had not yet arrived for him to exercise the limitless power that he thought needful, he declined an offer of reëlection from the provincial legislature, in the hope that, through a policy of conciliation, his successor might fall a prey to the designs of the Unitaries. When this happened, he secretly stirred up the provinces into a renewal of the earlier disturbances, until the evidence became overwhelming that Rosas alone could bring peace and progress out of turmoil and backwardness. Reluctantly the legislature yielded him the power it knew he wanted. This he would not accept until a "popular" vote of some 9000 to 4 confirmed the choice. In 1835, accordingly, he became dictator for the first of four successive terms of five years.

Then ensued, notably in Buenos Aires itself, a state of affairs at once grotesque and frightful. Not content with hunting down and inflicting every possible outrage upon those suspected of sympathy with the Unitaries, Rosas forbade them to display the light blue and white colors of their party device and directed that red, the sign of Federalism, should be displayed on all occasions. Pink he would not tolerate as being too attenuated a shade and altogether too suggestive of political trimming! A band of his followers, made up of ruffians, and called the *Mazorca,* or "Ear of Corn," because of the resemblance of their close fellowship to its adhering grains, broke into private houses, destroyed everything light blue within reach, and maltreated the unfortunate occupants at will. No man was safe also who did not give his face a leonine aspect by wearing a mustache and side-whiskers — emblems, the one of "federalism," and the other of "independence." To possess a visage bare of these hirsute adornments or a countenance too efflorescent in that respect was, under a régime of tonsorial politics, to invite personal disaster! Nothing apparently was too cringing or servile to show how submissive the people were to the mastery of Rosas. Private vengeance and defamation of the innocent did their sinister work unchecked. Even when his arbitrary treatment of foreigners had compelled France for a while to institute a blockade of Buenos Aires, the wily dictator utilized the incident to turn patriotic resentment to his own advantage.

Meanwhile matters in Uruguay had come to such a pass that Rosas saw an opportunity to extend his control in that direction also. Placed between Brazil and the Argentine Confederation and so often a bone of contention, the little country was hardly free from the rule of the former state when it came near falling under the domination of the latter. Only a few years of relative tranquillity had elapsed when two parties sprang up in Uruguay: the "Reds" (*Colorados*) and the "Whites" (*Blancos*). Of these, the one was supposed to represent the liberal and the other the conservative element. In fact, they were the followings of partisan chieftains, whose struggles for the presidency during many years to come retarded the advancement of a country to which nature had been generous.

When Fructuoso Rivera, the President up to 1835, thought of choosing some one to be elected in constitutional fashion as his successor, he unwisely singled out Manuel Oribe, one of the famous "Thirty-three" who had raised the cry of independence a decade before. But instead of a henchman he found a rival. Both of them straightway adopted the colors and bid for the support of one of the local factions; and both appealed to the factions of the Argentine Confederation for aid, Rivera to the Unitaries and Oribe to the Federalists. In 1843, Oribe, at the head of an army of *Blancos* and Federalists and with the moral support of Rosas, laid siege to Montevideo. Defended by *Colorados*, Unitaries, and numerous foreigners, including Giuseppe Garibaldi, the town held out valiantly for eight years — a feat that earned for it the title of the "New Troy." Anxious to stop the slaughter and destruction that were injuring their nationals, France, Great Britain, and Brazil offered their mediation; but Rosas would have none of it. What the antagonists did he cared little, so long as they enfeebled the country and increased his chances of dominating it. At length, in 1845, the two European powers established a blockade of Argentine ports, which was not lifted until the dictator grudgingly agreed to withdraw his troops from the neighboring republic.

More than any other single factor, this intervention of France and Great Britain administered a blow to Rosas from which he could not recover. The operations of their fleets and the resistance of Montevideo had lowered the prestige of the dictator and had raised the hopes of the Unitaries that a last desperate effort might shake off his hated control. In May, 1851, Justo José de Urquiza, one of his most trusted lieutenants, declared the independence of his own province and called upon the others to rise against the tyrant. Enlisting the support of Brazil, Uruguay, and Paraguay, he assembled a "great army of liberation," composed of about twenty-five thousand men, at whose head he marched to meet the redoubtable Rosas. On February 3, 1852, at a spot near Buenos Aires, the man of might who, like his contemporary Francia in Paraguay, had held the Argentine Confederation in thralldom for so many years, went down to final defeat. Embarking on a British warship he sailed for England, there to become a quiet country gentleman in a land where *gauchos* and dictators were unhonored.

In the meantime Paraguay, spared from such

convulsion as racked its neighbor on the east, dragged on its secluded existence of backwardness and stagnation. Indians and half-castes vegetated in ignorance and docility, and the handful of whites quaked in terror, while the inexorable Francia tightened the reins of commercial and industrial restriction and erected forts along the frontiers to keep out the pernicious foreigner. At his death, in 1840, men and women wept at his funeral in fear perchance, as one historian remarks, lest he come back to life; and the priest who officiated at the service likened the departed dictator to Cæsar and Augustus!

Paraguay was destined, however, to fall under a despot far worse than Francia when in 1862 Francisco Solano López became President. The new ruler was a man of considerable intelligence and education. While a traveler in Europe he had seen much of its military organizations, and he had also gained no slight acquaintance with the vices of its capital cities. This acquired knowledge he joined to evil propensities until he became a veritable monster of wickedness. Vain, arrogant, reckless, absolutely devoid of scruple, swaggering in victory, dogged in defeat, ferociously cruel at all times, he murdered his brothers and his best friends; he executed, imprisoned, or banished any one whom he thought too influential; he tortured his mother and sisters; and, like the French Terrorists, he impaled his officers upon the unpleasant dilemma of winning victories or losing their lives. Even members of the American legation suffered torment at his hands, and the minister himself barely escaped death.

Over his people, López wielded a marvelous power, compounded of persuasive eloquence and brute force. If the Paraguayans had obeyed their earlier masters blindly, they were dumb before this new despot and deaf to other than his word of command. To them he was the "Great Father," who talked to them in their own tongue of Guaraní, who was the personification of the nation, the greatest ruler in the world, the invincible champion who inspired them with a loathing and contempt for their enemies. Such were the traits of a man and such the traits of a people who waged for six years a warfare among the most extraordinary in human annals.

What prompted López to embark on his career of international madness and prosecute it with the rage of a demon is not entirely clear. A vision of himself as the Napoleon of southern South

America, who might cause Brazil, Argentina, and Uruguay to cringe before his footstool, while he disposed at will of their territory and fortunes, doubtless stirred his imagination. So, too, the thought of his country, wedged in between two huge neighbors and threatened with suffocation between their overlapping folds, may well have suggested the wisdom of conquering overland a highway to the sea. At all events, he assembled an army of upwards of ninety thousand men, the greatest military array that Hispanic America had ever seen. Though admirably drilled and disciplined, they were poorly armed, mostly with flintlock muskets, and they were also deficient in artillery except that of antiquated pattern. With this mighty force at his back, yet knowing that the neighboring countries could eventually call into the field armies much larger in size equipped with repeating rifles and supplied with modern artillery, the "Jupiter of Paraguay" nevertheless made ready to launch his thunderbolt.

The primary object at which he aimed was Uruguay. In this little state the *Colorados*, upheld openly or secretly by Brazil and Argentina, were conducting a "crusade of liberty" against the *Blanco* government at Montevideo, which was favored by Paraguay. Neither of the two great powers wished to see an alliance formed between Uruguay and Paraguay, lest when united in this manner the smaller nations might become too strong to tolerate further intervention in their affairs. For her part, Brazil had motives for resentment arising out of boundary disputes with Paraguay and Uruguay, as well as out of the inevitable injury to its nationals inflicted by the commotions in the latter country; whereas Argentina cherished grievances against López for the audacity with which his troops roamed through her provinces and the impudence with which his vessels, plying on the lower Paraná, ignored the customs regulations. Thus it happened that obscure civil discords in one little republic exploded into a terrific international struggle which shook South America to its foundations.

In 1864, scorning the arts of diplomacy which he did not apparently understand, López sent down an order for the two big states to leave the matter of Uruguayan politics to his impartial adjustment. At both Rio de Janeiro and Buenos Aires a roar of laughter went up from the press at this notion of an obscure chieftain of a band of Indians in the tropical backwoods daring to poise the equilibrium of much more than half a continent on his insolent hand. But the merriment soon subsided, as Brazilians and Argentinos came to realize what their peril might be from a huge army of skilled and valiant soldiers, a veritable horde of fighting fanatics, drawn up in a compact little land, centrally located and affording in other respects every kind of strategic advantage.

When Brazil invaded Uruguay and restored the *Colorados* to power, López demanded permission from Argentina to cross its frontier, for the purpose of assailing his enemy from another quarter. When the permission was denied, López declared war on Argentina also. It was in every respect a daring step, but López knew that Argentina was not so well prepared as his own state for a war of endurance. Uruguay then entered into an alliance in 1865 with its two big "protectors." In accordance with its terms, the allies agreed not to conclude peace until López had been overthrown, heavy indemnities had been exacted of Paraguay, its fortifications demolished, its army disbanded, and the country forced to accept any boundaries that the victors might see fit to impose.

Into the details of the campaigns in the frightful conflict that ensued it is not necessary to enter.

Although, in 1866, the allies had assembled an army of some fifty thousand men, López continued taking the offensive until, as the number and determination of his adversaries increased, he was compelled to retreat into his own country. Here he and his Indian legions levied terrific toll upon the lives of their enemies who pressed onward, up or down the rivers and through tropical swamps and forests. Inch by inch he contested their entry upon Paraguayan soil. When the able-bodied men gave out, old men, boys, women, and girls fought on with stubborn fury, and died before they would surrender. The wounded escaped if they could, or, cursing their captors, tore off their bandages and bled to death. Disease wrought awful havoc in all the armies engaged; yet the struggle continued until flesh and blood could endure no more. Flying before his pursuers into the wilds of the north and frantically dragging along with him masses of fugitive men, women, and children, whom he remorselessly shot, or starved to death, or left to perish of exhaustion, López turned finally at bay, and, on March 1, 1870, was felled by the lance of a cavalryman. He had sworn to die for his country and he did, though his country might perish with him.

No land in modern times has ever reached a

point so near annihilation as Paraguay. Added to the utter ruin of its industries and the devastation of its fields, dwellings, and towns, hundreds of thousands of men, women, and children had perished. Indeed, the horrors that had befallen it might well have led the allies to ask themselves whether it was worth while to destroy a country in order to change its rulers. Five years before López came into power the population of Paraguay had been reckoned at something between 800,000 and 1,400,000 — so unreliable were census returns in those days. In 1873 it was estimated at about 230,000, of whom women over fifteen years of age outnumbered the men nearly four to one. Loose polygamy was the inevitable consequence, and women became the breadwinners. Even today in this country the excess of females over males is very great. All in all, it is not strange that Paraguay should be called the "Niobe among nations."

Unlike many nations of Spanish America in which a more or less anticlerical régime was in the ascendant, Ecuador fell under a sort of theocracy. Here appeared one of the strangest characters in a story already full of extraordinary personages — Gabriel García Moreno, who became President of that republic in 1861. In some respects the counterpart of Francia of Paraguay, in others both a medieval mystic and an enlightened ruler of modern type, he was a man of remarkable intellect, constructive ability, earnest patriotism, and disinterested zeal for orderliness and progress. On his presidential sash were inscribed the words: "My Power in the Constitution"; but his real power lay in himself and in the system which he implanted.

García Moreno had a varied career. He had been a student of chemistry and other natural sciences. He had spent his youth in exile in Europe, where he prepared himself for his subsequent career as a journalist and a university professor. Through it all he had been an active participant in public affairs. Grim of countenance, austere in bearing, violent of temper, relentless in severity, he was a devoted believer in the Roman Catholic faith and in this Church as the sole effective basis upon which a state could be founded or social and political regeneration could be assured. In order to render effective his concept of what a nation ought to be, García Moreno introduced and upheld in all rigidity an administration the like of which had been known hardly anywhere since the Middle Ages. He recalled the Jesuits, established schools of the "Brothers of the Christian Doctrine," and made education a matter wholly under ecclesiastical control. He forbade heretical worship, called the country the "Republic of the Sacred Heart," and entered into a concordat with the Pope under which the Church in Ecuador became more subject to the will of the supreme pontiff than western Europe had been in the days of Innocent III.

Liberals in and outside of Ecuador tried feebly to shake off this masterful theocracy, for the friendship which García Moreno displayed toward the diplomatic representatives of the Catholic powers of Europe, notably those of Spain and France, excited the neighboring republics. Colombia, indeed, sent an army to liberate the "brother democrats of Ecuador from the rule of Professor García Moreno," but the mass of the people stood loyally by their President. For this astounding obedience to an administration apparently so unrelated to modern ideas, the ecclesiastical domination was not solely or even chiefly responsible. In more ways than one García Moreno, the professor President, was a statesman of vision and deed. He put down brigandage and lawlessness; reformed the finances; erected hospitals; promoted education; and encouraged the study of natural science.

Even his salary he gave over to public improvements. His successors in the presidential office found it impossible to govern the country without García Moreno. Elected for a third term to carry on his curious policy of conservatism and reaction blended with modern advancement, he fell by the hand of an assassin in 1875. But the system which he had done so much to establish in Ecuador survived him for many years.

Although Brazil did not escape the evils of insurrection which retarded the growth of nearly all of its neighbors, none of its numerous commotions shook the stability of the nation to a perilous degree. By 1850 all danger of revolution had vanished. The country began to enter upon a career of peace and progress under a régime which combined broadly the federal organization of the United States with the form of a constitutional monarchy. Brazil enjoyed one of the few enlightened despotisms in South America. Adopting at the outset the parliamentary system, the Emperor Pedro II chose his ministers from among the liberals or conservatives, as one party or the other might possess a majority in the lower house of the Congress. Though the legislative power of the nation was enjoyed almost entirely by the planters and their associates who formed the dominant social class, individual liberty was fully guaranteed, and even freedom of conscience and of the press was allowed. Negro slavery, though tolerated, was not expressly recognized.

Thanks to the political discretion and unusual personal qualities of "Dom Pedro," his popularity became more and more marked as the years went on. A patron of science and literature, a scholar rather than a ruler, a placid and somewhat eccentric philosopher, careless of the trappings of state, he devoted himself without stint to the public welfare. Shrewdly divining that the monarchical system might not survive much longer, he kept his realm pacified by a policy of conciliation. Pedro II even went so far as to call himself the best republican in the Empire. He might have said, with justice perhaps, that he was the best republican in the whole of Hispanic America. What he really accomplished was the successful exercise of a paternal autocracy of kindness and liberality over his subjects.

If more or less permanent dictators and occasional liberators were the order of the day in most of the Spanish American republics, intermittent dictators and liberators dashed across the stage in Mexico from 1829 well beyond the middle of the century. The other countries could show numerous instances in which the occupant of the chief magistracy held office to the close of his constitutional term; but Mexico could not show a single one! What Mexico furnished, instead, was a kaleidoscopic spectacle of successive presidents or dictators, an unstable array of self-styled "generals" without a presidential succession. There were no fewer than fifty such transient rulers in thirty-two years, with anywhere from one to six a year, with even the same incumbent twice in one year, or, in the case of the repetitious Santa Anna, nine times in twenty years — in spite of the fact that the constitutional term of office was four years. This was a record that made the most turbulent South American states seem, by comparison, lands of methodical regularity in the choice of their national executive. And as if this instability in the chief magistracy were not enough, the form of government in Mexico shifted violently from federal to centralized, and back again to federal. Mad struggles raged between partisan chieftains and their bands of *Escoceses* and *Yorkinos*, crying out upon the "President" in power because of his undue influence upon the choice of a successor, backing their respective candidates if they lost, and waiting for a chance to oust them if they won.

This tumultuous epoch had scarcely begun when Spain in 1829 made a final attempt to recover her lost dominion in Mexico. Local quarrels were straightway dropped for two months until the invaders had surrendered. Thereupon the great landholders, who disliked the prevailing *Yorkino* régime for its democratic policies and for favoring the abolition of slavery, rallied to the aid of a "general" who issued a manifesto demanding an observance of the constitution and the laws! After Santa Anna, who was playing the rôle of a Mexican Warwick, had disposed of this aspirant, he switched blithely over to the *Escoceses*, reduced the federal system almost to a nullity, and in 1836 marched away to conquer the revolting Texans. But, instead, they conquered him and gained their independence, so that his reward was exile.

Now the *Escoceses* were free to promulgate a new constitution, to abolish the federal arrangement altogether, and to replace it by a strongly centralized government under which the individual States became mere administrative districts.

Hardly had this radical change been effected when in 1838 war broke out with France on account of the injuries which its nationals, among whom were certain pastry cooks, had suffered during the interminable commotions. Mexico was forced to pay a heavy indemnity; and Santa Anna, who had returned to fight the invader, was unfortunate enough to lose a leg in the struggle. This physical deprivation, however, did not interfere with that doughty hero's zest for tilting with other unquiet spirits who yearned to assure national regeneration by continuing to elevate and depose "presidents."

Another swing of the political pendulum had restored the federal system when again everything was overturned by the disastrous war with the United States. Once more Santa Anna returned, this time, however, to joust in vain with the "Yankee despoilers" who were destined to dismember Mexico and to annex two-thirds of its territory. Again Santa Anna was banished — to dream of a more favorable opportunity when he might become the savior of a country which had fallen into bankruptcy and impotence.

His opportunity came in 1853, when conservatives and clericals indulged the fatuous hope that he would both sustain their privileges and lift

Mexico out of its sore distress. Either their memories were short or else distance had cast a halo about his figure. At all events, he returned from exile and assumed, for the ninth and last time, a presidency which he intended to be something more than a mere dictatorship. Scorning the formality of a Congress, he had himself entitled "Most Serene Highness," as indicative of his ambition to become a monarch in name as well as in fact.

Royal or imperial designs had long since brought one military upstart to grief. They were now to cut Santa Anna's residence in Mexico similarly short. Eruptions of discontent broke out all over the country. Unable to make them subside, Santa Anna fell back upon an expedient which recalls practices elsewhere in Spanish America. He opened registries in which all citizens might record "freely" their approval or disapproval of his continuance in power. Though he obtained the huge majority of affirmative votes to be expected in such cases, he found that these pen-and-ink signatures were no more serviceable than his soldiers. Accordingly the dictator of many a day, fallen from his former estate of highness, decided to abandon his serenity also, and in 1854 fled the country — for its good and his own.

CHAPTER VI

PERIL FROM ABROAD

APART from the spoliation of Mexico by the United States, the independence of the Hispanic nations had not been menaced for more than thirty years. Now comes a period in which the plight of their big northern neighbor, rent in twain by civil war and powerless to enforce the spirit of the Monroe Doctrine, caused two of the countries to become subject a while to European control. One of these was the Dominican Republic.

In 1844 the Spanish-speaking population of the eastern part of the island of Santo Domingo, writhing under the despotic yoke of Haiti, had seized a favorable occasion to regain their freedom. But the magic word "independence" could not give stability to the new state any more than it had done in the case of its western foes. The Haitians had lapsed long since into a condition resembling that of their African forefathers. They reveled in the barbarities of Voodoo, a sort of snake worship, and they groveled before "presidents" and "emperors" who rose and fell on the tide of decaying civilization. The Dominicans unhappily were not much more progressive. Revolutions alternated with invasions and counterinvasions and effectually prevented enduring progress.

On several occasions the Dominicans had sought reannexation to Spain or had craved the protection of France as a defense against continual menace from their negro enemies and as a relief from domestic turmoil. But every move in this direction failed because of a natural reluctance on the part of Spain and France, which was heightened by a refusal of the United States to permit what it regarded as a violation of the Monroe Doctrine. In 1861, however, the outbreak of civil war in the United States appeared to present a favorable opportunity to obtain protection from abroad. If the Dominican Republic could not remain independent anyway, reunion with the old mother country seemed altogether preferable to reconquest by Haiti. The President, therefore, entered into negotiations with the Spanish Governor and Captain General of Cuba, and then issued a proclamation signed by himself and four of his ministers announcing that by the "free and spontaneous will" of its citizens, who had conferred upon him the power to do so, the nation recognized Queen Isabella II as its lawful sovereign! Practically no protest was made by the Dominicans against this loss of their independence.

Difficulties which should have been foreseen by Spain were quick to reveal themselves. It fell to the ex-President, now a colonial governor and captain general, to appoint a host of officials and, not unnaturally, he named his own henchmen. By so doing he not only aroused the animosity of the disappointed but stimulated that of the otherwise disaffected as well, until both the aggrieved factions began to plot rebellion. Spain, too, sent over a crowd of officials who could not adjust themselves to local conditions. The failure of the mother country to allow the Dominicans representation in the Spanish Cortes and its readiness to levy taxes stirred up resentment that soon ended in revolution. Unable to check this new trouble, and awed by the threatening attitude of the United States, Spain decided to withdraw in 1865. The Dominicans thus were left with their independence and a chance — which they promptly seized — to renew their commotions. So serious did these disturbances become that in 1869 the President of the reconstituted republic sought annexation to the United States but without success. American efforts, on the other hand, were equally futile to restore peace and order in the troubled country until many years later.

The intervention of Spain in Santo Domingo and its subsequent withdrawal could not fail to have disastrous consequences in its colony of Cuba, the "Pearl of the Antilles" as it was proudly called. Here abundant crops of sugar and tobacco had brought wealth and luxury, but not many immigrants because of the havoc made by epidemics of yellow fever. Nearly a third of the insular population was still composed of negro slaves, who could hardly relish the thought that, while the mother country had tolerated the suppression of the hateful institution in Santo Domingo, she still maintained it in Cuba. A bureaucracy, also, prone to corruption owing to the temptations of loose accounting at the custom house, governed in routinary, if not in arbitrary, fashion. Under these circumstances dislike for the suspicious and repressive administration of Spain grew apace, and secret societies renewed their agitation for its overthrow.

The symptoms of unrest were aggravated by the forced retirement of Spain from Santo Domingo. If the Dominicans had succeeded so well, it ought not to be difficult for a prolonged rebellion to wear Spain out and compel it to abandon Cuba also. At this critical moment news was brought of a Spanish revolution across the seas.

Just as the plight of Spain in 1808, and again in 1820, had afforded a favorable opportunity for its colonies on the continents of America to win their independence, so now in 1868 the tidings that Queen Isabella had been dethroned by a liberal uprising aroused the Cubans to action under their devoted leader, Carlos Manuel de Céspedes. The insurrection had not gained much headway, however, when the provisional government of the mother country instructed a new Governor and Captain General — whose name, Dulce (Sweet), had an auspicious sound — to open negotiations with the insurgents and to hold out the hope of reforms. But the royalists, now as formerly, would listen to no compromise. Organizing themselves into bodies of volunteers, they drove Dulce out. He was succeeded by one Caballero de Rodas (Knight of Rhodes) who lived up to his name by trying to ride roughshod over the rebellious Cubans. Thus began the Ten Years' War — a war of skirmishes and brief encounters, rarely involving a decisive action, which drenched the soil of Cuba with blood and laid waste its fields in a fury of destruction.

Among the radicals and liberals who tried to retain a fleeting control over Mexico after the final departure of Santa Anna was the first genuine statesman it had ever known in its history as a republic — Benito Pablo Juárez, an Indian. At twelve years of age he could not read or write or even speak Spanish. His employer, however, noted his intelligence and had him educated. Becoming a lawyer, Juárez entered the political arena and rose to prominence by dint of natural talent for leadership, an indomitable perseverance, and a sturdy patriotism. A radical by conviction, he felt that the salvation of Mexico could never be attained until clericalism and militarism had been banished from its soil forever.

Under his influence a provisional government had already begun a policy of lessening the privileges of the Church, when the conservative elements, with a cry that religion was being attacked, rose up in arms again. This movement repressed, a Congress proceeded in 1857 to issue a liberal constitution which was destined to last for sixty years. It established the federal system in a definite fashion, abolished special privileges, both ecclesiastical and military, and organized the country on sound bases worthy of a modern nation. Mexico seemed about to enter upon a rational development. But the newly elected President, yielding to the importunities of the clergy, abolished the constitution, dissolved the legislature, and set up a dictatorship, in spite of the energetic protests of Juárez, who had been chosen Chief Justice of the Supreme Court, and who, in accordance with the terms of the temporarily discarded instrument, was authorized to assume the presidency should that office fall vacant. The rule of the usurper was short-lived, however. Various improvised "generals" of conservative stripe put themselves at the head of a movement to "save country, religion, and the rights of the army," drove the would-be dictator out, and restored the old régime.

Juárez now proclaimed himself acting President, as he was legally entitled to do, and set up his government at Vera Cruz while one "provisional president" followed another. Throughout this trying time Juárez defended his position vigorously and rejected every offer of compromise. In

1859 he promulgated his famous Reform Laws which nationalized ecclesiastical property, secularized cemeteries, suppressed religious communities, granted freedom of worship, and made marriage a civil contract. For Mexico, however, as for other Spanish American countries, measures of the sort were far too much in advance of their time to insure a ready acceptance. Although Juárez obtained a great moral victory when his government was recognized by the United States, he had to struggle two years more before he could gain possession of the capital. Triumphant in 1861, he carried his anticlerical program to the point of actually expelling the Papal Nuncio and other ecclesiastics who refused to obey his decrees. By so doing he leveled the way for the clericals, conservatives, and militarists to invite foreign intervention on behalf of their desperate cause. But, even if they had not been guilty of behavior so unpatriotic, the anger of the Pope over the treatment of his Church, the wrath of Spain over the conduct of Juárez, who had expelled the Spanish minister for siding with the ecclesiastics, the desire of Great Britain to collect debts due to her subjects, and above all the imperialistic ambitions of Napoleon III, who dreamt of converting the intellectual influence of France in Hispanic America into a political ascendancy, would probably have led to European occupation in any event, so long at least as the United States was split asunder and incapable of action.

Some years before, the Mexican Government under the clerical and militarist régime had made a contract with a Swiss banker who for a payment of $500,000 had received bonds worth more than fifteen times the value of the loan. When, therefore, the Mexican Congress undertook to defer payments on a foreign debt that included the proceeds of this outrageous contract, the Governments of France, Great Britain, and Spain decided to intervene. According to their agreement the three powers were simply to hold the seaports of Mexico and collect the customs duties until their pecuniary demands had been satisfied. Learning, however, that Napoleon III had ulterior designs, Great Britain and Spain withdrew their forces and left him to proceed with his scheme of conquest. After capturing Puebla in May, 1863, a French army numbering some thirty thousand men entered the capital and installed an assemblage of notables belonging to the clerical and conservative groups. This body thereupon proclaimed the establishment of a constitutional monarchy under an emperor. The title was to be offered to Maximilian, Archduke of Austria. In case he should not accept, the matter was to be referred to the "benevolence of his majesty, the Emperor of the French," who might then select some other Catholic prince.

On his arrival, a year later, the amiable and well-meaning Maximilian soon discovered that, instead of being an "Emperor," he was actually little more than a precarious chief of a faction sustained by the bayonets of a foreign army. In the northern part of Mexico, Juárez, Porfirio Díaz, — later to become the most renowned of presidential autocrats, — and other patriot leaders, though hunted from place to place, held firmly to their resolve never to bow to the yoke of the pretender. Nor could Maximilian be sure of the loyalty of even his supposed adherents. Little by little the unpleasant conviction intruded itself upon him that he must either abdicate or crush all resistance in the hope that eventually time and good will might win over the Mexicans. But do what they would, his foreign legions could not catch the wary and stubborn Juárez and his guerrilla lieutenants, who persistently wore down the forces of their enemies. Then the financial situation became grave. Still more menacing was the attitude of the United States now that its civil war was at an end. On May 31, 1866, Maximilian received word that Napoleon III had decided to withdraw the French troops. He then determined to abdicate, but he was restrained by the unhappy Empress Carlotta, who hastened to Europe to plead his cause with Napoleon. Meantime, as the French troops were withdrawn, Juárez occupied the territory.

Feebly the "Emperor" strove to enlist the favor of his adversaries by a number of liberal decrees; but their sole result was his abandonment by many a lukewarm conservative. Inexorably the patriot armies closed around him until in May, 1867, he was captured at Querétaro, where he had sought refuge. Denied the privilege of leaving the country on a promise never to return, he asked Escobedo, his captor, to treat him as a prisoner of war. "That's my business," was the grim reply. On the pretext that Maximilian had refused to recognize the competence of the military court chosen to try him, Juárez gave the order to shoot him. On the 19th of June the Austrian archduke paid for a fleeting glory with his life. Thus failed the second attempt at erecting an empire in Mexico. For thirty-four years diplomatic relations between that country and Austria-Hungary were severed. The clerical-military combination had been overthrown, and the Mexican people had reaffirmed their independence. As Juárez declared: "Peace means respect for the rights of others."

Even if foreign dreams of empire in Mexico had vanished so abruptly, it could hardly be expected that a land torn for many years by convulsions could become suddenly tranquil. With Díaz and other aspirants to presidential power, or with chieftains who aimed at setting up little republics of their own in the several states, Juárez had to contend for some time before he could establish a fair amount of order. Under his successor, who also was a civilian, an era of effective reform began. In 1873 amendments to the constitution declared Church and State absolutely separate and provided for the abolition of peonage — a provision which was more honored in the breach than in the observance.

CHAPTER VII

GREATER STATES AND LESSER

During the half century that had elapsed since 1826, the nations of Hispanic America had passed through dark ages. Their evolution had always been accompanied by growing pains and had at times been arrested altogether or unduly hastened by harsh injections of radicalism. It was not an orderly development through gradual modifications in the social and economic structure, but rather a fitful progress now assisted and now retarded by the arbitrary deeds of men of action, good and bad, who had seized power. Dictators, however, steadily decreased in number and gave place often to presidential autocrats who were continued in office by constant reëlection and who were imbued with modern ideas. In 1876 these Hispanic nations stood on the threshold of a new era. Some were destined to advance rapidly beyond it; others, to move slowly onward; and a few to make little or no progress.

The most remarkable feature in the new era was the rise of four states — Mexico, Brazil, Argentina, and Chile — to a position of eminence among their fellows. Extent of territory, development of natural resources, the character of the inhabitants and the increase of their numbers, and the amount of popular intelligence and prosperity, all contributed to this end. Each of the four nations belonged to a fairly well-defined historical and geographical group in southern North America, and in eastern and western South America, respectively. In the first group were Mexico, the republics of Central America, and the island countries of the Caribbean; in the second, Brazil, Argentina, Uruguay, and Paraguay; and in the third, Chile, Peru, and Bolivia. In a fourth group were Ecuador, Colombia, and Venezuela.

When the President of Mexico proceeded, in 1876, to violate the constitution by securing his reëlection, the people were prepared by their earlier experiences and by the rule of Juárez to defend their constitutional rights. A widespread rebellion headed by Díaz broke out. In the so-called "Plan of Tuxtepec" the revolutionists declared themselves in favor of the principle of absolutely no reëlection.

Meantime the Chief Justice of the Supreme Court handed down a decision that the action of the Congress in sustaining the President was illegal, since in reality no elections had been held because of the abstention of voters and the seizure of the polls by revolutionists or government forces. "Above the constitution, nothing; above the constitution, no one," he declared. But as this assumption of a power of judgment on matters of purely political concern was equally a violation of the constitution and concealed, besides, an attempt to make the Chief Justice President, Díaz and his followers drove both of the pretenders out. Then in 1876 he managed to bring about his own election instead.

Porfirio Díaz was a soldier who had seen active service in nearly every important campaign since the war with the United States. Often himself in revolt against presidents, legal and illegal, Díaz was vastly more than an ordinary partisan chieftain. Schooled by a long experience, he had come to appreciate the fact that what Mexico required for its national development was freedom from internal disorders and a fair chance for recuperation. Justice, order, and prosperity, he felt, could be assured only by imposing upon the country the heavy weight of an iron hand. Foreign capital must be invested in Mexico and then protected; immigration must be encouraged, and other material, moral, and intellectual aid of all sorts must be drawn from abroad for the upbuilding of the nation.

To effect such a transformation in a land so tormented and impoverished as Mexico — a country which, within the span of fifty-five years had lived under two "emperors," and some thirty-six presidents, nine "provisional presidents," ten dictators, twelve "regents," and five "supreme councilors" — required indeed a masterful intelligence and a masterful authority. Porfirio Díaz possessed and exercised both. He was, in fact, just the man for the times. An able administrator, stern and severe but just, rather reserved in manner and guarded in utterance, shrewd in the selection of associates, and singularly successful in his dealings with foreigners, he entered upon a "presidential reign" of thirty-five years — broken by but one intermission of four — which brought Mexico out upon the highway to new national life.

Under the stable and efficient rulership of Díaz, "plans," "pronunciamentos," "revolutions," and similar devices of professional trouble makers, had short shrift. Whenever an uprising started, it was promptly quelled, either by a well-disciplined army or by the *rurales*, a mounted police made up to some extent of former bandits to whom the President gave the choice of police service or of sharp punishment for their crimes. Order, in fact, was not always maintained, nor was justice always meted out, by recourse to judges and courts. Instead, a novel kind of lynch law was invoked. The name it bore was the *ley fuga*, or "flight law," in accordance with which malefactors or political suspects taken by government agents from one locality to another, on the excuse of securing readier justice, were given by their captors a pretended chance to escape and were then shot while they ran! The only difference between this method and others of the sort employed by Spanish American autocrats to enforce obedience lay in its purpose. Of Díaz one might say what Bacon said of King Henry VII: "He drew blood as physicians do, to save life rather than to spill it." If need be, here and there, disorder and revolt were stamped out by terrorism; but the Mexican people did not yield to authority from terror but rather from a thorough loyalty to the new régime.

Among the numerous measures of material improvement which Díaz undertook during his first term, the construction of railways was the most important. The size of the country, its want of navigable rivers, and its relatively small and widely scattered population, made imperative the establishment of these means of communication. Despite the misgivings of many intelligent Mexicans that the presence of foreign capital would impair local independence in some way, Díaz laid the foundations of future national prosperity by granting concessions to the Mexican Central and National Mexican companies, which soon began construction. Under his successor a national bank was created; and when Díaz was again elected he readjusted the existing foreign debt and boldly contracted new debts abroad.

At the close of his first term, in 1880, a surplus in the treasury was not so great a novelty as the circumstance — altogether unique in the political annals of Mexico — that Díaz turned over the presidency in peaceful fashion to his properly elected successor! He did so reluctantly, to be sure, but he could not afford just yet to ignore his own avowed principle, which had been made a part of the constitution shortly after his accession. Although the confidence he reposed in that successor was not entirely justified, the immense personal popularity of Díaz saved the prestige of the new chief magistrate. Under his administration the constitution was amended in such a way as to deprive the Chief Justice of the privilege of replacing the President in case of a vacancy, thus eliminating that official from politics. After his resumption of office, Díaz had the fundamental law modified anew, so as to permit the reelection of a President for one term only! For this change, inconsistent though it may seem, Díaz was not alone responsible. Circumstances had changed, and the constitution had to change with them.

Had the "United Provinces of Central America," as they came forth from under the rule of Spain, seen fit to abstain from following in the unsteady footsteps of Mexico up to the time of the accession of Díaz to power, had they done nothing more than develop their natural wealth and utilize their admirable geographical situation, they might have become prosperous and kept their corporate name. As it was, their history for upwards of forty years had little to record other than a momentary cohesion and a subsequent lapse into five quarrelsome little republics — the "Balkan States" of America. Among them Costa Rica had suffered least from arbitrary management or internal commotion and showed the greatest signs of advancement.

In Guatemala, however, there had arisen another Díaz, though a man quite inferior in many respects to his northern counterpart. When Justo Rufino Barrios became President of that republic in 1873 he was believed to have conservative leanings. Ere long, however, he astounded his compatriots by showing them that he was a thoroughgoing radical with methods of action to correspond to his convictions. Not only did he keep the Jesuits out of the country but he abolished monastic orders altogether and converted their buildings to public use. He made marriage a civil contract and he secularized the burying grounds. Education he encouraged by engaging the services of foreign instructors, and he brought about a better observance of the law by the promulgation of new codes. He also introduced railways and telegraph lines. Since the manufacture of aniline dyes abroad had diminished the demand for cochineal, Barrios decided to replace this export by cultivating coffee. To this end, he distributed seeds among the planters and furnished financial aid besides, with a promise to inspect the fields in due season and see what had been accomplished. Finding that in many cases the seeds had been thrown away and the money wasted in drink and gambling, he ordered the guilty planters to be given fifty lashes, with the assurance that on a second offense he would shoot them on sight. Coffee planting in Guatemala was pursued thereafter with much alacrity!

Posts in the government service Barrios distributed quite impartially among Conservatives and Democrats, deserving or otherwise, for he had them both well under control. At his behest a permanent constitution was promulgated in 1880. While he affected to dislike continual reëlection, he saw to it nevertheless that he himself should be the sole candidate who was likely to win.

Barrios doubtless could have remained President of Guatemala for the term of his natural life if he had not raised up the ghost of federation. All the republics of Central America accepted his invitation in 1876 to send delegates to his capital to discuss the project. But nothing was accomplished because Barrios and the President of Salvador were soon at loggerheads. Nine years later, feeling himself stronger, Barrios again proposed federation. But the other republics had by this time learned too much of the methods of the autocrat of Guatemala, even while they admired his progressive policy, to relish the thought of a federation dominated by Guatemala and its masterful President. Though he "persuaded" Honduras to accept the plan, the three other republics preferred to unite in self-defense, and in the ensuing struggle the quixotic Barrios was killed. A few years later the project was revived and the constitution of a "Republic of Central America" was agreed upon, when war between Guatemala and Salvador again frustrated its execution.

In Brazil two great movements were by this time under way: the total abolition of slavery and the establishment of a republic. Despite the tenacious opposition of many of the planters, from about the year 1883 the movement for emancipation made great headway. There was a growing determination on the part of the majority of the inhabitants to remove the blot that made the country an object of reproach among the civilized states of the world. Provinces and towns, one after another, freed the slaves within their borders. The imperial Government, on its part, hastened the process by liberating its own slaves and by imposing upon those still in bondage taxes higher than their market value; it fixed a price for other slaves; it decreed that the older slaves should be set free; and it increased the funds already appropriated to compensate owners of slaves who should be emancipated. In 1887 the number of slaves had fallen to about 720,000, worth legally about $650 each. A year later came the final blow, when the Princess Regent assented to a measure which abolished slavery outright and repealed all former acts relating to slavery. So radical a proceeding wrought havoc in the coffee-growing southern provinces in particular, from which the negroes now freed migrated by tens of thousands to the northern provinces. Their places, however, were taken by Italians and other Europeans who came to work the plantations on a coöperative basis. All through the eighties, in fact, immigrants from Italy poured into the temperate regions of southern Brazil, to the number of nearly two hundred thousand, supplementing the many thousands of Germans who had settled, chiefly in the province of Rio Grande do Sul, thirty years before.

Apart from the industrial problem thus created by the abolition of slavery, there seemed to be no serious political or economic questions before the country. Ever since 1881, when a law providing for direct elections was passed, the Liberals had been in full control. The old Dom Pedro, who had endeared himself to his people, was as much liked and respected as ever. But as he had grown feeble and almost blind, the heiress to the throne, who had marked absolutist and clerical tendencies, was disposed to take advantage of his infirmities.

For many years, on the other hand, doctrines opposed to the principle of monarchy had been spread in zealous fashion by members of the military class, notable among whom was Deodoro da Fonseca. And now some of the planters longed to wreak vengeance on a ruler who had dared to thwart their will by emancipating the slaves. Besides this persistent discontent, radical republican newspapers continually stirred up fresh agitation. Whatever the personal service rendered by the Emperor to the welfare of the country, to them he represented a political system which deprived the provinces of much of their local autonomy and the Brazilian people at large of self-government.

But the chief reason for the momentous change which was about to take place was the fact that the constitutional monarchy had really completed its work as a transitional government. Under that régime Brazil had reached a condition of stability and had attained a level of progress which might well enable it to govern itself. During all this time the influence of the Spanish American nations had been growing apace. Even if they had fallen into many a political calamity, they were nevertheless "republics," and to the South American this word had a magic sound. Above all, there was the potent suggestion of the success of the United States of North America, whose extension of its federal system over a vast territory suggested what Brazil with its provinces might accomplish in the southern continent. Hence the vast majority of intelligent Brazilians felt that they had become self-reliant enough to establish a republic without fear of lapsing into the unfortunate experiences of the other Hispanic countries.

In 1889, when provision was made for a speedy abdication of the Emperor in favor of his daughter, the republican newspapers declared that a scheme was being concocted to exile the chief military agitators and to interfere with any effort on the part of the army to prevent the accession of the new ruler. Thereupon, on the 15th of November, the radicals at Rio de Janeiro, aided by the garrison, broke out in open revolt. Proclaiming the establishment of a federal republic under the name of the "United States of Brazil," they deposed the imperial ministry, set up a provisional government with Deodoro da Fonseca at its head, arranged for the election of a constitutional convention, and bade Dom Pedro and his family leave the country within twenty-four hours.

On the 17th of November, before daybreak, the summons was obeyed. Not a soul appeared to bid the old Emperor farewell as he and his family boarded the steamer that was to bear them to exile in Europe. Though seemingly an act of heartlessness and ingratitude, the precaution was a wise one in that it averted possible conflict and bloodshed. For the second time in its history, a fundamental change had been wrought in the political system of the nation without a resort to war! The United States of Brazil accordingly took its place peacefully among its fellow republics of the New World.

Meanwhile Argentina, the great neighbor of Brazil to the southwest, had been gaining territory and new resources. Since the definite adoption of a federal constitution in 1853, this state had attained to a considerable degree of national consciousness under the leadership of able presidents such as Bartolomé Mitre, the soldier and historian, and Domingo Faustino Sarmiento, the publicist and promoter of popular education. One evidence of this new nationalism was a widespread belief in the necessity of territorial expansion. Knowing that Chile entertained designs upon Patagonia, the Argentine Government forestalled any action by conducting a war of practical extermination against the Indian tribes of that region and by adding it to the national domain. The so-called "conquest of the desert" in the far south of the continent opened to civilization a vast habitable area of untold economic possibilities.

In the electoral campaign of 1880 the presidential candidates were Julio Argentino Roca and the Governor of the province of Buenos Aires. The former, an able officer skilled in both arms and politics, had on his side the advantage of a reputation won in the struggle with the Patagonian Indians, the approval of the national Government, and the support of most of the provinces. Feeling certain of defeat at the polls, the partisans of the latter candidate resorted to the timeworn expedient of a revolt. Though the uprising lasted but twenty days, the diplomatic corps at the capital proffered its mediation between the contestants, in order to avoid any further bloodshed. The result was that the fractious Governor withdrew his candidacy and a radical change was effected in the relations of Buenos Aires, city and province, to the country at large. The city, together with its environs, was converted into a federal district and became solely and distinctively the national capital. Its public buildings, railways, and telegraph service, as well as the provincial debt, were taken over by the general Government. The seat of provincial authority was transferred to the village of Ensenada, which thereupon was rechristened La Plata.

A veritable tide of wealth and general prosperity was now rolling over Argentina. By 1885 its population had risen to upwards of 3,000,000. Immigration increased to a point far beyond the wildest expectations. In 1889 alone about 300,000 newcomers arrived and lent their aid in the promotion of industry and commerce. Fields hitherto uncultivated or given over to grazing now bore vast crops of wheat, maize, linseed, and sugar. Large quantities of capital, chiefly from Great Britain, also poured into the country. As a result, the price of land rose high, and feverish speculation became the order of the day. Banks and other institutions of credit were set up, colonizing schemes were devised, and railways were laid out. To meet the demands of all these enterprises, the Government borrowed immense sums from foreign capitalists and issued vast quantities of paper money, with little regard for its ultimate redemption. Argentina spent huge sums in prodigal fashion on all sorts of public improvements in an effort to attract still more capital and immigration, and thus entered upon a dangerous era of inflation.

Of the near neighbors of Argentina, Uruguay continued along the tortuous path of alternate disturbance and progress, losing many of its inhabitants to the greater states beyond, where they sought relative peace and security; while Paraguay, on the other hand, enjoyed freedom from civil strife, though weighed down with a war debt and untold millions in indemnities exacted by Argentina and Brazil, which it could never hope to pay. In consequence, this indebtedness was a useful club to brandish over powerless Paraguay whenever that little country might venture to question the right of either of its big neighbors to break the promise they had made of keeping its territory intact. Argentina, however, consented in 1878 to refer certain claims to the decision of the President of the United States. When Paraguay won the arbitration, it showed its gratitude by naming one of its localities Villa Hayes. As time went on, however, its population increased and hid many of the scars of war.

On the western side of South America there broke out the struggle known as the "War of the Pacific" between Chile, on the one side, and Peru and Bolivia as allies on the other. In Peru unstable and corrupt governments had contracted foreign loans under conditions that made their repayment almost impossible and had spent the proceeds in so reckless and extravagant a fashion as to bring the country to the verge of bankruptcy. Bolivia, similarly governed, was still the scene of the orgies and carnivals which had for some time characterized its unfortunate history. One of its buffoon "presidents," moreover, had entered into boundary agreements with both Chile and Brazil, under which the nation lost several important areas and some of its territory on the Pacific. The boundaries of Bolivia, indeed, were run almost everywhere on purely arbitrary lines drawn with scant regard for the physical features of the country and with many a frontier question left wholly unsettled.

For some years Chilean companies and speculators, aided by foreign capital mainly British in origin, had been working deposits of nitrate of soda in the province of Antofagasta, or "the desert of Atacama," a region along the coast to the northward belonging to Bolivia, and also in the provinces of Tacna, Arica, and Tarapacá, still farther to the northward, belonging to Peru. Because boundary lines were not altogether clear and because the three countries were all eager to exploit these deposits, controversies over this debatable ground were sure to rise. For the privilege of developing portions of this region, individuals and companies had obtained concessions from the various governments concerned; elsewhere, industrial free lances dug away without reference to such formalities.

It is quite likely that Chile, whose motto was "By Right or by Might," was prepared to sustain the claims of its citizens by either alternative. At all events, scenting a prospective conflict, Chile had devoted much attention to the development of its naval and military establishment — a state of affairs which did not escape the observation of its suspicious neighbors.

The policy of Peru was determined partly by personal motives and partly by reasons of state.

In 1873 the President, lacking sufficient financial and political support to keep himself in office, resolved upon the risky expedient of arousing popular passion against Chile, in the hope that he might thereby replenish the national treasury. Accordingly he proceeded to pick a quarrel by ordering the deposits in Tarapacá to be expropriated with scant respect for the concessions made to the Chilean miners. Realizing, however, the possible consequences of such an action, he entered into an alliance with Bolivia. This country thereupon proceeded to levy an increased duty on the exportation of nitrates from the Atacama region. Chile, already aware of the hostile combination which had been formed, protested so vigorously that a year later Bolivia agreed to withdraw the new regulations and to submit the dispute to arbitration.

Such were the relations of these three states in 1878, when Bolivia, taking advantage of differences of opinion between Chile and Argentina regarding the Patagonian region, reimposed its export duty, canceled the Chilean concessions, and confiscated the nitrate deposits. Chile then declared war in February, 1879, and within two months occupied the entire coast of Bolivia up to the frontiers of Peru. On his part the President of Bolivia was too much engrossed in the festivities connected with a masquerade to bother about notifying the people that their land had been invaded until several days after the event had occurred!

Misfortunes far worse than anything which had fallen to the lot of its ally now awaited Peru, which first attempted an officious mediation and then declared war on the 4th of April. Since Peru and Bolivia together had a population double that of Chile, and since Peru possessed a much larger army and navy than Chile, the allies counted confidently on victory. But Peru's army of eight thousand — having within four hundred as many officers as men, directed by no fewer than twenty-six generals, and presided over by a civil government altogether inept — was no match for an army less than a third of its size to be sure, but well drilled and commanded, and with a stable, progressive, and efficient government at its back. The Peruvian forces, lacking any substantial support from Bolivia, crumpled under the terrific attacks of their adversaries. Efforts on the part of the United States to mediate in the struggle were blocked by the dogged refusal of Chile to abate its demands for annexation. Early in 1881 its army entered Lima in triumph, and the war was over.

For a while the victors treated the Peruvians and their capital city shamefully. The Chilean soldiers stripped the national library of its contents, tore up the lamp-posts in the streets, carried away the benches in the parks, and even shipped off the local menagerie to Santiago! What they did not remove or destroy was disposed of by the rabble of Lima itself. But in two years so utterly chaotic did the conditions in the hapless country become that Chile at length had to set up a government in order to conclude a peace. It was not until October 20, 1883, that the treaty was signed at Lima and ratified later at Ancón. Peru was forced to cede Tarapacá outright and to agree that Tacna and Arica should be held by Chile for ten years. At the expiration of this period the inhabitants of the two provinces were to be allowed to choose by vote the country to which they would prefer to belong, and the nation that won the election was to pay the loser 10,000,000 *pesos*. In April, 1884, Bolivia, also, entered into an arrangement with Chile, according to which a portion of its seacoast should be ceded absolutely and the remainder should be occupied by

Chile until a more definite understanding on the matter could be reached.

Chile emerged from the war not only triumphant over its northern rivals but dominant on the west coast of South America. Important developments in Chilean national policy followed. To maintain its vantage and to guard against reprisals, the victorious state had to keep in military readiness on land and sea. It therefore looked to Prussia for a pattern for its army and to Great Britain for a model for its navy.

Peru had suffered cruelly from the war. Its territorial losses deprived it of an opportunity to satisfy its foreign creditors through a grant of concessions. The public treasury, too, was empty, and many a private fortune had melted away. Not until a military hand stronger than its competitors managed to secure a firm grip on affairs did Peru begin once more its toilsome journey toward material betterment.

Bolivia, on its part, had emerged from the struggle practically a landlocked country. Though bereft of access to the sea except by permission of its neighbors, it had, however, not endured anything like the calamities of its ally. In 1880 it had adopted a permanent constitution and it now entered upon a course of slow and relatively peaceful progress.

In the republics to the northward struggles between clericals and radicals caused sharp, abrupt alternations in government. In Ecuador the hostility between clericals and radicals was all the more bitter because of the rivalry of the two chief towns, Guayaquil the seaport and Quito the capital, each of which sheltered a faction. No sooner therefore had García Moreno fallen than the radicals of Guayaquil rose up against the clericals at Quito. Once in power, they hunted their enemies down until order under a dictator could be restored. The military President who assumed power in 1876 was too radical to suit the clericals and too clerical to suit the radicals. Accordingly his opponents decided to make the contest three-cornered by fighting the dictator and one another. When the President had been forced out, a conservative took charge until parties of bushwhackers and mutinous soldiers were able to install a military leader, whose retention of power was brief. In 1888 another conservative, who had been absent from the country when elected and who was an adept in law and diplomacy, managed to win sufficient support from all three factions to retain office for the constitutional period.

In Colombia a financial crisis had been approaching ever since the price of coffee, cocoa, and other Colombian products had fallen in the European markets. This decrease had caused a serious diminution in the export trade and had forced gold and silver practically out of circulation. At the same time the various "states" were increasing their powers at the expense of the federal Government, and the country was rent by factions. In order to give the republic a thoroughly centralized administration which would restore financial confidence and bring back the influence of the Church as a social and political factor, a genuine revolution, which was started in 1876, eventually put an end to both radicalism and states' rights. At the outset Rafael Núñez, the unitary and clerical candidate and a lawyer by profession, was beaten on the field, but at a subsequent election he obtained the requisite number of votes and, in 1880, assumed the presidency. That the loser in war should become the victor in peace showed the futility of bloodshed in such revolutions.

Not until Núñez came into office again did he feel himself strong enough to uproot altogether the radicalism and disunion which had flourished since 1860. Ignoring the national Legislature, he called a Congress of his own, which in 1886 framed a constitution that converted the "sovereign states" into "departments," or mere administrative districts, to be ruled as the national Government saw fit. Further, the presidential term was lengthened from two years to six, and the name of the country was changed, finally, to "Republic of Colombia." Two years later the power of the Church was strengthened by a concordat with the Pope.

Venezuela on its part had undergone changes no less marked. A liberal constitution promulgated in 1864 had provided for the reorganization of the country on a federal basis. The name chosen for the republic was "United States of Venezuela." More than that, it had anticipated Mexico and Guatemala in being the first of the Hispanic nations to witness the establishment of a presidential autocracy of the continuous and enlightened type.

Antonio Guzmán Blanco was the man who imposed upon Venezuela for about nineteen years a régime of obedience to law, and, to some extent, of modern ideas of administration such as the country had never known before. A person of much versatility, he had studied medicine and law before he became a soldier and a politician. Later he displayed another kind of versatility by letting henchmen hold the presidential office while he remained the power behind the throne. Endowed with a masterful will and a pronounced taste for minute supervision, he had exactly the ability necessary to rule Venezuela wisely and well.

Amid considerable opposition he began, in 1870, the first of his three periods of administration —the *Septennium*, as it was termed. The "sovereign" states he governed through "sovereign" officials of his own selection. He stopped the plundering of farms and the dragging of laborers off to military service. He established in Venezuela an excellent monetary system. Great sums were expended in the erection of public and private buildings and in the embellishment of Caracas. European capital and immigration were encouraged to venture into a country hitherto so torn by chronic disorder as to deprive both labor and property of all guarantees. Roads, railways, and telegraph lines were constructed. The ministers of the Church were rendered submissive to the civil power. Primary education became alike free and compulsory. As the phrase went, Guzmán Blanco "taught Venezuela to read." At the end of his term of office he went into voluntary retirement.

In 1879 Guzmán Blanco put himself at the head of a movement which he called a "revolution of replevin" — which meant, presumably, that he was opposed to presidential "continuism," and in favor of republican institutions! Although a constitution promulgated in 1881 fixed the chief magistrate's term of office at two years, the success which Guzmán Blanco had attained enabled him to control affairs for five years — the *Quinquennium*, as it was called. Thereupon he procured his appointment to a diplomatic post in Europe; but the popular demand for his presence was too strong for him to remain away. In 1886 he was elected by acclamation. He held office two years more and then, finding that his influence had waned, he left Venezuela for good. Whatever his faults in other respects, Guzmán Blanco — be it said to his credit — tried to destroy the pest of periodical revolutions in his country. Thanks to his vigorous suppression of these uprisings, some years of at least comparative security were made possible. More than any other President the nation had ever had, he was entitled to the distinction of having been a benefactor, if not altogether a regenerator, of his native land.

CHAPTER VIII

"ON THE MARGIN OF INTERNATIONAL LIFE"

DURING the period from 1889 to 1907 two incidents revealed the standing that the republics of Hispanic America had now acquired in the world at large. In 1889 at Washington, and later in their own capital cities, they met with the United States in council. In 1899, and again in 1907, they joined their great northern neighbor and the nations of Europe and Asia at The Hague for deliberation on mutual concerns, and they were admitted to an international fellowship and coöperation far beyond a mere recognition of their independence and a formal interchange of diplomats and consuls.

Since attempts of the Hispanic countries themselves to realize the aims of Bolívar in calling the Congress at Panamá had failed, the United States now undertook to call into existence a sort of inter-American Congress. Instead of being merely a supporter, the great republic of the north had resolved to become the director of the movement for greater solidarity in thought and action. By linking up the concerns of the Hispanic nations with its own destinies it would assert not so much its position as guardian of the Monroe Doctrine as its headship, if not its actual dominance, in the New World, and would so widen the bounds of its political and commercial influence — a tendency known as "imperialism." Such was the way, at least, in which the Hispanic republics came to view the action of the "Colossus of the North" in inviting them to participate in an assemblage meeting more or less periodically and termed officially the "International Conference of American States," and popularly the "Pan-American Conference."

Whether the mistrust the smaller countries felt at the outset was lessened in any degree by the attendance of their delegates at the sessions of this conference remains open to question. Although these representatives, in common with their colleagues from the United States, assented to a variety of conventions and passed a much larger number of resolutions, their acquiescence seemed due to a desire to gratify their powerful associate, rather than to a belief in the possible utility of such measures. The experience of the earlier gatherings had demonstrated that political issues would have to be excluded from consideration. Propositions, for example, such as that to extend the basic idea of the Monroe Doctrine into a sort of self-denying ordinance, under which all the nations of America should agree to abstain thereafter from acquiring any part of one another's territory by conquest, and to adopt, also, the principle of compulsory arbitration, proved impossible of acceptance. Accordingly, from that time onward the matters treated by the Conference dealt for the most part with innocuous, though often praiseworthy, projects for bringing the United States and its sister republics into closer commercial, industrial, and intellectual relations.

The gathering itself, on the other hand, became to a large extent a *fiesta*, a festive occasion for the display of social amenities. Much as the Hispanic Americans missed their favorite topic of politics, they found consolation in entertaining the distinguished foreign visitors with the genial courtesy and generous hospitality for which they are famous. As one of their periodicals later expressed it, since a discussion of politics was tabooed, it were better to devote the sessions of the Conference to talking about music and lyric poetry! At all events, as far as the outcome was concerned, their national legislatures ratified comparatively few of the conventions.

Among the Hispanic nations of America only Mexico took part in the First Conference at The Hague. Practically all of them were represented at the second. The appearance of their delegates at these august assemblages of the powers of earth was viewed for a while with mixed feelings. The attitude of the Great Powers towards them resembled that of parents of the old régime: children at the international table should be "seen and not heard." As a matter of fact, the Hispanic Americans were both seen and heard — especially the latter! They were able to show the Europeans that, even if they did happen to come from relatively weak states, they possessed a skillful intelligence, a breadth of knowledge, a capacity for expression, and a consciousness of national character, which would not allow them simply to play "Man Friday" to an international Crusoe. The president of the second conference, indeed, confessed that they had been a "revelation" to him.

Hence, as time went on, the progress and possibilities of the republics of Hispanic America came to be appreciated more and more by the world at large. Gradually people began to realize that the countries south of the United States were not merely an indistinguishable block on the map, to be referred to vaguely as "Central and South America" or as "Latin America." The reading public at least knew that these countries were quite different from one another, both in achievements and in prospects.

Yet the fact remains that, despite their active part in these American and European conferences, the Hispanic countries of the New World did not receive the recognition which they felt was their due. Their national associates in the European gatherings were disinclined to admit that the possession of independence and sovereignty entitled them to equal representation on international council boards. To a greater or less degree, therefore, they continued to stay in the borderland where no one either affirmed or denied their individuality. To quote the phrase of an Hispanic American, they stood "on the margin of international life." How far they might pass beyond it into the full privileges of recognition and association on equal terms, would depend upon the readiness with which they could atone for the errors or recover from the misfortunes of the past, and upon their power to attain stability, prosperity, strength, and responsibility.

Certain of the Hispanic republics, however, were not allowed to remain alone on their side of "the margin of international life." Though nothing so extreme as the earlier French intervention took place, foreign nations were not at all averse to crossing over the marginal line and teaching them what a failure to comply with international obligations meant. The period from 1889 to 1907, therefore, is characterized also by interference on the part of European powers, and by interposition on the part of the United States, in the affairs of countries in and around the Caribbean Sea. Because of the action taken by the United States two more republics — Cuba and Panamá — came into being, thus increasing the number of political offshoots from Spain in America to eighteen. Another result of this interposition was the creation of what were substantially American protectorates. Here the United States did not deprive the countries concerned of their independence and sovereignty, but subjected them to a kind of guardianship or tutelage, so far as it thought needful to insure stability, solvency, health, and welfare in general.

Foremost in the northern group of Hispanic nations, Mexico, under the guidance of Díaz, marched steadily onward. Peace, order, and law; an increasing population; internal wealth and well-being; a flourishing industry and commerce; suitable care for things mental as well as material; the respect and confidence of foreigners — these were blessings which the country had hitherto never beheld. The Mexicans, once in anarchy and enmity created by militarists and clericals, came to know one another in friendship, and arrived at something like a national consciousness.

In 1889 there was held the first conference on educational problems which the republic had ever had. Three years later a mining code was drawn up which made ownership inviolable on payment of lawful dues, removed uncertainties of operation, and stimulated the industry in a remarkable fashion. Far less beneficial in the long run was a law enacted in 1894. Instead of granting a legal title to lands held by prescriptive rights through an occupation of many years, it made such property part of the public domain, which might be acquired, like a mining claim, by any one who could secure a grant of it from the Government. Though hailed at the time as a piece of constructive legislation, its unfortunate effect was to enable large landowners who wished to increase their possessions to oust poor cultivators of the soil from their humble holdings. On the other hand, under the statesmanlike management of José Yves Limantour, the Minister of Finance, the monetary situation at home and abroad was strengthened beyond measure, and banking interests were promoted accordingly. Further, an act abolishing the *alcabala*, a vexatious internal revenue tax, gave a great stimulus to freedom of commerce throughout the country. In order to insure a continuance of the new régime, the constitution was altered in three important respects. The amendment of 1890 restored the original clause of 1857, which permitted indefinite reëlection to the presidency; that of 1896 established a presidential succession in case of a vacancy, beginning with the Minister of Foreign Affairs; and that of 1904 lengthened the term of the chief magistrate from four years to six and created the office of Vice President.

In Central America two republics, Guatemala and Costa Rica, set an excellent example both because they were free from internal commotions and because they refrained from interference in the affairs of their neighbors. The contrast between these two quiet little nations, under their lawyer Presidents, and the bellicose but equally small Nicaragua, Honduras, and Salvador, under their chieftains, military and juristic, was quite remarkable. Nevertheless another attempt at confederation was made. In 1895 the ruler of Honduras, declaring that reunion was a "primordial necessity," invited his fellow potentates of Nicaragua and Salvador to unite in creating the "Greater Republic of Central America" and asked Guatemala and Costa Rica to join. Delegates actually appeared from all five republics, attended *fiestas*, gave expression to pious wishes, and went home! Later still, in 1902, the respective Presidents signed a "convention of peace and obligatory arbitration" as a means of adjusting perpetual disagreements about politics and boundaries; but nothing was done to carry these ideas into effect.

The personage mainly responsible for these failures was José Santos Zelaya, one of the most arrant military lordlets and meddlers that Central America had produced in a long time. Since 1893 he had been dictator of Nicaragua, a country not only entangled in continuous wrangles among its towns and factions, but bowed under an enormous burden of debt created by excessive emissions of paper money and by the contraction of more or less scandalous foreign loans. Quite undisturbed by the financial situation, Zelaya promptly silenced local bickerings and devoted his energies to altering the constitution for his presidential benefit and to making trouble for his neighbors. Nor did he refrain from displays of arbitrary conduct that were sure to provoke foreign intervention. Great Britain, for example, on two occasions exacted reparation at the cannon's mouth for ill treatment of its citizens.

Zelaya waxed wroth at the spectacle of Guatemala, once so active in revolutionary arts but now quietly minding its own business. In 1906, therefore, along with parties of Hondurans, Salvadoreans, and disaffected Guatemalans, he began an invasion of that country and continued operations with decreasing success until, the United States and Mexico offering their mediation, peace was signed aboard an American cruiser. Then, when Costa Rica invited the other republics to discuss confederation within its calm frontiers, Zelaya preferred his own particular occupation to any such procedure. Accordingly, displeased with a recent boundary decision, he started along with Salvador to fight Honduras. Once more the United States and Mexico tendered their good offices, and again a Central American conflict was closed aboard an American warship. About the only real achievement of Zelaya was the signing of a treaty by which Great Britain recognized the complete sovereignty of Nicaragua over the Mosquito Indians, whose buzzing for a larger amount of freedom and more tribute had been disturbing unduly the "repose" of that small nation!

To the eastward the new republic of Cuba was about to be born. Here a promise of adequate representation in the Spanish Cortes and of a local legislature had failed to satisfy the aspirations of many of its inhabitants. The discontent was aggravated by lax and corrupt methods of administration as well as by financial difficulties. Swarms of Spanish officials enjoyed large salaries without performing duties of equivalent value. Not a few of them had come over to enrich themselves at public expense and under conditions altogether scandalous. On Cuba, furthermore, was saddled the debt incurred by the Ten Years' War, while the island continued to be a lucrative market for Spanish goods without obtaining from Spain a corresponding advantage for its own products.

As the insistence upon a removal of these abuses

and upon a grant of genuine self-government became steadily more clamorous, three political groups appeared. The Constitutional Unionists, or "Austrianizers," as they were dubbed because of their avowed loyalty to the royal house of Bourbon-Hapsburg, were made up of the Spanish and conservative elements and represented the large economic interests and the Church. The Liberals, or "Autonomists," desired such reforms in the administration as would assure the exercise of self-government and yet preserve the bond with the mother country. On the other hand, the Radicals, or "Nationalists" — the party of "Cuba Free" — would be satisfied with nothing short of absolute independence. All these differences of opinion were sharpened by the activities of a sensational press.

From about 1890 onward the movement toward independence gathered tremendous strength, especially when the Cubans found popular sentiment in the United States so favorable to it. Excitement rose still higher when the Spanish Government proposed to bestow a larger measure of autonomy. When, however, the Cortes decided upon less liberal arrangements, the Autonomists declared that they had been deceived, and the

Nationalists denounced the utter unreliability of Spanish promises. Even if the concessions had been generous, the result probably would have been the same, for by this time the plot to set Cuba free had become so widespread, both in the island itself and among the refugees in the United States, that the inevitable struggle could not have been deferred.

In 1895 the revolution broke out. The whites, headed by Máximo Gómez, and the negroes and mulattoes by their chieftain, Antonio Macéo, both of whom had done valiant service in the earlier war, started upon a campaign of deliberate terrorism. This time they were resolved to win at any cost. Spurning every offer of conciliation, they burned, ravaged, and laid waste, spread desolation along their pathway, and reduced thousands to abject poverty and want.

Then the Spanish Government came to the conclusion that nothing but the most rigorous sort of reprisals would check the excesses of the rebels. In 1896 it commissioned Valeriano Weyler, an officer who personified ferocity, to put down the rebellion. If the insurgents had fancied that the conciliatory spirit hitherto displayed by the Spaniards was due to irresolution or weakness, they found that these were not the qualities of their new opponent. Weyler, instead of trying to suppress the rebellion by hurrying detachments of troops first to one spot and then to another in pursuit of enemies accustomed to guerrilla tactics, determined to stamp it out province by province. To this end he planted his army firmly in one particular area, prohibited the planting or harvesting of crops there, and ordered the inhabitants to assemble in camps which they were not permitted to leave on any pretext whatever. This was his policy of "reconcentration." Deficient food supply, lack of sanitary precautions, and absence of moral safeguards made conditions of life in these camps appalling. Death was a welcome relief. Reconcentration, combined with executions and deportations, could have but one result—the "pacification" of Cuba by converting it into a desert.

Not in the United States alone but in Spain itself the story of these drastic measures kindled popular indignation to such an extent that, in 1897, the Government was forced to recall the ferocious Weyler and to send over a new Governor and Captain General, with instructions to abandon the worst features of his predecessor's policy and to establish a complete system of autonomy in both

Cuba and Porto Rico. Feeling assured, however, that an ally was at hand who would soon make their independence certain, the Cuban patriots flatly rejected these overtures. In their expectations they were not mistaken. By its armed intervention, in the following year the United States acquired Porto Rico for itself and compelled Spain to withdraw from Cuba.[1]

The island then became a republic, subject only to such limitations on its freedom of action as its big guardian might see fit to impose. Not only was Cuba placed under American rule from 1899 to 1902, but it had to insert in the Constitution of 1901 certain clauses that could not fail to be galling to Cuban pride. Among them two were of special significance. One imposed limitations on the financial powers of the Government of the new nation, and the other authorized the United States, at its discretion, to intervene in Cuban affairs for the purpose of maintaining public order. The Cubans, it would seem, had exchanged a dependence on Spain for a restricted independence measured by the will of a country infinitely stronger.

Cuba began its life as a republic in 1902, under

[1] See *The Path of Empire*, by Carl Russell Fish (in *The Chronicles of America*).

a government for which a form both unitary and federal had been provided. Tomás Estrada Palma, the first President and long the head of the Cuban junta in the United States, showed himself disposed from the outset to continue the beneficial reforms in administration which had been introduced under American rule. Prudent and conciliatory in temperament, he tried to dispel as best he could the bitter recollections of the war and to repair its ravages. In this policy he was upheld by the conservative class, or Moderates. Their opponents, the Liberals, dominated by men of radical tendencies, were eager to assert the right, to which they thought Cuba entitled as an independent sovereign nation, to make possible mistakes and correct them without having the United States forever holding the ferule of the schoolmaster over it. They were well aware, however, that they were not at liberty to have their country pass through the tempestuous experience which had been the lot of so many Hispanic republics. They could vent a natural anger and disappointment, nevertheless, on the President and his supporters. Rather than continue to be governed by Cubans not to their liking, they were willing to bring about a renewal of American rule.

In this respect the wishes of the Radicals were soon gratified. Hardly had Estrada Palma, in 1906, assumed office for a second time, when parties of malcontents, declaring that he had secured his re-election by fraudulent means, rose up in arms and demanded that he annul the vote and hold a fair election. The President accepted the challenge and waged a futile conflict, and again the United States intervened. Upon the resignation of Estrada Palma, an American Governor was again installed, and Cuba was told in unmistakable fashion that the next intervention might be permanent.

Less drastic but quite as effectual a method of assuring order and regularity in administration was the action taken by the United States in another Caribbean island. A little country like the Dominican Republic, in which few Presidents managed to retain their offices for terms fixed by changeable constitutions, could not resist the temptation to rid itself of a ruler who had held power for nearly a quarter of a century. After he had been disposed of by assassination in 1899, the government of his successor undertook to repudiate a depreciated paper currency by ordering the customs duties to be paid in specie; and it also tried to prevent the consul of an aggrieved foreign nation from attaching certain revenues as security for the payment of the arrears of an indemnity. Thereupon, in 1905, the President of the United States entered into an arrangement with the Dominican Government whereby, in return for a pledge from the former country to guarantee the territorial integrity of the republic and an agreement to adjust all of its external obligations of a pecuniary sort, American officials were to take charge of the custom house and apportion the receipts from that source in such a manner as to satisfy domestic needs and pay foreign creditors.[1]

[1] See *The Path of Empire*, by Carl Russell Fish (in *The Chronicles of America*).

CHAPTER IX

THE REPUBLICS OF SOUTH AMERICA

EVEN so huge and conservative a country as Brazil could not start out upon the pathway of republican freedom without some unrest; but the political experience gained under a régime of limited monarchy had a steadying effect. Besides, the Revolution of 1889 had been effected by a combination of army officers and civilian enthusiasts who knew that the provinces were ready for a radical change in the form of government, but who were wise enough to make haste slowly. If a motto could mean anything, the adoption of the positivist device, "Order and Progress," displayed on the national flag seemed a happy augury.

The constitution promulgated in 1891 set up a federal union broadly similar to that of the United States, except that the powers of the general Government were somewhat more restricted. Qualifications for the suffrage were directly fixed in the fundamental law itself, but the educational tests imposed excluded the great bulk of the population from the right to vote. In the constitution, also, Church and State were declared absolutely separate, and civil marriage was prescribed.

Well adapted as the constitution was to the particular needs of Brazil, the Government erected under it had to contend awhile with political disturbances. Though conflicts occurred between the President and the Congress, between the federal authority and the States, and between the civil administration and naval and military officials, none were so constant, so prolonged, or so disastrous as in the Spanish American republics. Even when elected by the connivance of government officials, the chief magistrate governed in accordance with republican forms. Presidential power, in fact, was restrained both by the huge size of the country and by the spirit of local autonomy upheld by the States.

Ever since the war with Paraguay the financial credit of Brazil had been impaired. The chronic deficit in the treasury had been further increased by a serious lowering in the rate of exchange, which was due to an excessive issue of paper money. In order to save the nation from bankruptcy Manoel

Ferraz de Campos Salles, a distinguished jurist, was commissioned to effect an adjustment with the British creditors. As a result of his negotiations a "funding loan" was obtained, in return for which an equivalent amount in paper money was to be turned over for cancellation at a fixed rate of exchange. Under this arrangement depreciation ceased for awhile and the financial outlook became brighter.

The election of Campos Salles to the presidency in 1898, as a reward for his success, was accompanied by the rise of definite political parties. Among them the Radicals or Progressists favored a policy of centralization under military auspices and exhibited certain antiforeign tendencies. The Moderates or Republicans, on the contrary, with Campos Salles as their candidate, declared for the existing constitution and advocated a gradual adoption of such reforms as reason and time might suggest. When the latter party won the election, confidence in the stability of Brazil returned.

As if Uruguay had not already suffered enough from internal discords, two more serious conflicts demonstrated once again that this little country, in which political power had been held substantially by one party alone since 1865, could not hope for permanent peace until either the excluded and apparently irreconcilable party had been finally and utterly crushed, or, far better still, until the two factions could manage to agree upon some satisfactory arrangement for rotation in office. The struggle of 1897 ended in the assassination of the President and in a division of the republic into two practically separate areas, one ruled by the *Colorados* at Montevideo, the other by the *Blancos*. A renewal of civil war in 1904 seemed altogether preferable to an indefinite continuance of this dualism in government, even at the risk of friction with Argentina, which was charged with not having observed strict neutrality. This second struggle came to a close with the death of the insurgent leader; but it cost the lives of thousands and did irreparable damage to the commerce and industry of the country.

Uruguay then enjoyed a respite from party upheavals until 1910, when José Batlle, the able, resolute, and radical-minded head of the *Colorados*, announced that he would be a candidate for the presidency. As he had held the office before and had never ceased to wield a strong personal influence over the administration of his successor, the *Blancos* decided that now was the time to attempt once more to oust their opponents from the control which they had monopolized for half a century. Accusing the Government of an unconstitutional centralization of power in the executive, of preventing free elections, and of crippling the pastoral industries of the country, they started a revolt, which ran a brief course. Batlle proved himself equal to the situation and quickly suppressed the insurrection. Though he did make a wide use of his authority, the President refrained from indulging in political persecution and allowed the press all the liberty it desired in so far as was consistent with the law. It was under his direction that Uruguay entered upon a remarkable series of experiments in the nationalization of business enterprises. Further, more or less at the suggestion of Batlle, a new constitution was ratified by popular vote in 1917. It provided for a division of the executive power between the President and a National Council of Administration, forbade the election of administrative and military officials to the Congress, granted to that body a considerable increase of power, and enlarged the facilities for local self-government. In addition, it established the principle of minority representation and of secrecy of the ballot, permitted the Congress to extend the right of suffrage to women, and dissolved the union between Church and State. If the terms of the new instrument are faithfully observed, the old struggle between *Blancos* and *Colorados* will have been brought definitely to a close.

Paraguay lapsed after 1898 into the earlier sins of Spanish America. Upon a comparatively placid presidential régime followed a series of barrack uprisings or attacks by Congress on the executive. The constitution became a farce. No longer, to be sure, an abode of Arcadian seclusion as in colonial times, or a sort of territorial cobweb from the center of which a spiderlike Francia hung motionless or darted upon his hapless prey, or even a battle ground on which fanatical warriors might fight and die at the behest of a savage López, Paraguay now took on the aspect of an arena in which petty political gamecocks might try out their spurs. Happily, the opposing parties spent their energies in high words and vehement gestures rather than in blows and bloodshed. The credit of the country sank lower and lower until its paper money stood at a discount of several hundred per cent compared with gold.

European bankers had begun to view the financial future of Argentina also with great alarm. In

1890 the mad careering of private speculation and public expenditure along the roseate pathway of limitless credit reached a veritable "crisis of progress." A frightful panic ensued. Paper money fell to less than a quarter of its former value in gold. Many a firm became bankrupt, and many a fortune shriveled. As is usual in such cases, the Government had to shoulder the blame. A four-day revolution broke out in Buenos Aires, and the President became the scapegoat; but the panic went on, nevertheless, until gold stood at nearly five to one. Most of the banks suspended payment; the national debt underwent a huge increase; and immigration practically ceased.

By 1895, however, the country had more or less resumed its normal condition. A new census showed that the population had risen to four million, about a sixth of whom resided in the capital. The importance which agriculture had attained was attested by the establishment of a separate ministry in the presidential cabinet. Industry, too, made such rapid strides at this time that organized labor began to take a hand in politics. The short-lived "revolution" of 1905, for example, was not primarily the work of politicians but of strikers organized into a workingmen's federation.

For three months civil guarantees were suspended, and by a so-called "law of residence," enacted some years before and now put into effect, the Government was authorized to expel summarily any foreigner guilty of fomenting strikes or of disturbing public order in any other fashion.

Political agitation soon assumed a new form. Since the Autonomist-National party had been in control for thirty years or more, it seemed to the Civic-Nationalists, now known as Republicans, to the Autonomists proper, and to various other factions, that they ought to do something to break the hold of that powerful organization. Accordingly in 1906 the President, supported by a coalition of these factions, started what was termed an "upward-downward revolution" — in other words, a series of interventions by which local governors and members of legislatures suspected of Autonomist-National leanings were to be replaced by individuals who enjoyed the confidence of the Administration. Pretexts for such action were not hard to find under the terms of the constitution; but their political interests suffered so much in the effort that the promoters had to abandon it.

Owing to persistent obstruction on the part of Congress, which took the form of a refusal either to sanction his appointments or to approve the budget, the President suspended the sessions of that body in 1908 and decreed a continuance of the estimates for the preceding year. The antagonism between the chief executive and the legislature became so violent that, if his opponents had not been split up into factions, civil war might have ensued in Argentina.

To remedy a situation made worse by the absence — usual in most of the Hispanic republics — of a secret ballot and by the refusal of political malcontents to take part in elections, voting was made both obligatory and secret in 1911, and the principle of minority representation was introduced. Legislation of this sort was designed to check bribery and intimidation and to enable the radical-minded to do their duty at the polls. Its effect was shown five years later, when the secret ballot was used substantially for the first time. The radicals won both the presidency and a majority in the Congress.

One of the secrets of the prosperity of Argentina, as of Brazil, in recent years has been its abstention from warlike ventures beyond its borders and its endeavor to adjust boundary conflicts by arbitration. Even when its attitude toward its huge neighbor had become embittered in consequence of a boundary decision rendered by the President of the United States in 1895, it abated none of its enthusiasm for the principle of a peaceful settlement of international disputes. Four years later, in a treaty with Uruguay, the so-called "Argentine Formula" appeared. To quote its language: "The contracting parties agree to submit to arbitration all questions of any nature which may arise between them, provided they do not affect provisions of the constitution of either state, and cannot be adjusted by direct negotiation." This Formula was soon put to the test in a serious dispute with Chile.

In the Treaty of 1881, in partitioning Patagonia, the crest of the Andes had been assumed to be the true continental watershed between the Atlantic and the Pacific and hence was made the boundary line between Argentina and Chile. The entire Atlantic coast was to belong to Argentina, the Pacific coast to Chile; the island of Tierra del Fuego was to be divided between them. At the same time the Strait of Magellan was declared a neutral waterway, open to the ships of all nations. Ere long, however, it was ascertained that the crest of the Andes did not actually coincide with the continental divide. Thereupon Argentina insisted that the boundary line should be made to run along the crest, while Chile demanded that it be traced along the watershed. Since the mountainous area concerned was of little value, the question at bottom was simply one of power and prestige between rival states.

As the dispute waxed warmer, a noisy press and populace clamored for war. The Governments of the two nations spent large sums in increasing their armaments; and Argentina, in imitation of its western neighbor, made military service compulsory. But, as the conviction gradually spread that a struggle would leave the victor as prostrate as the vanquished, wiser counsels prevailed. In 1899, accordingly, the matter was referred to the King of Great Britain for decision. Though the award was a compromise, Chile was the actual gainer in territory.

By their treaties of 1902 both republics declared their intention to uphold the principle of arbitration and to refrain from interfering in each other's affairs along their respective coasts. They also agreed upon a limitation of armaments — the sole example on record of a realization of the purpose of the First Hague Conference. To commemorate still further their international accord, in 1904 they erected on the summit of the Uspallata Pass, over which San Martín had crossed with his army of liberation in 1817, a bronze statue of Christ the Redeemer. There, amid the snow-capped peaks of the giant Andes, one may read inscribed upon the pedestal: "Sooner shall these mountains crumble to dust than Argentinos and Chileans break the peace which at the feet of Christ the Redeemer they have sworn to maintain!" Nor has the peace been broken.

Though hostilities with Argentina had thus been averted, Chile had experienced within its own frontiers the most serious revolution it had known in sixty years. The struggle was not one of partisan chieftains or political groups but a genuine contest to determine which of two theories of government should prevail — the presidential or the parliamentary, a presidential autocracy with the spread of real democracy or a congressional oligarchy based on the existing order. The sincerity and public spirit of both contestants helped to lend dignity to the conflict.

José Manuel Balmaceda, a man of marked ability, who became President in 1886, had devoted much of his political life to urging an enlargement of the executive power, a greater freedom to municipalities in the management of their local affairs, and a broadening of the suffrage. He had even advocated a separation of Church and State. Most of these proposals so conservative a land as Chile was not prepared to accept. Though civil marriage was authorized and ecclesiastical influence was lessened in other respects, the Church stood firm. During his administration Balmaceda introduced many reforms, both material and educational. He gave a great impetus to the construction of public works, enhanced the national credit by a favorable conversion of the public debt, fostered immigration, and devoted especial attention to the establishment of secondary schools.

Excellent as the administration of Balmaceda had been in other respects, he nevertheless failed to combine the liberal factions into a party willing to support the plans of reform which he had steadily favored. The parliamentary system made Cabinets altogether unstable, as political groups in the lower house of the Congress alternately cohered and fell apart. This defect, Balmaceda thought, should be corrected by making the members of his official family independent of the legislative branch. The Council of State, a somewhat anomalous body placed between the President and Cabinet on the one side and the Congress on the other, was an additional obstruction to a smooth-running administration. For it he would substitute a tribunal charged with the duty of resolving conflicts between the two chief branches of government. Balmaceda believed, also, that greater liberty should be given to the press and that existing taxes should be altered as rarely as possible. On its side, the Congress felt that the President was trying to establish a dictatorship and to replace the unitary system by a federal union, the probable weakness of which would enable him to retain his power more securely.

Toward the close of his term in January, 1891, when the Liberals declined to support his candidate for the presidency, Balmaceda, furious at the opposition which he had encountered, took matters into his own hands. Since the Congress refused to pass the appropriation bills, he declared that body dissolved and proceeded to levy the taxes by decree. To this arbitrary and altogether unconstitutional performance the Congress retorted by declaring the President deposed. Civil war broke out forthwith, and a strange spectacle presented itself. The two chief cities, Santiago and Valparaiso, and most of the army backed Balmaceda, whereas the country districts, especially in the north, and practically all the navy upheld the Congress.

These were, indeed, dark days for Chile. During a struggle of about eight months the nation suffered more than it had done in years of warfare with Peru and Bolivia. Though the bulk of the army stood by Balmaceda, the Congress was able to raise and organize a much stronger fighting force under a Prussian drillmaster. The tide of battle turned; Santiago and Valparaiso capitulated; and the presidential cause was lost. Balmaceda, who had taken refuge in the Argentina legation, committed suicide. But the Balmacedists, who were included in a general amnesty, still maintained themselves as a party to advocate in a peaceful fashion the principles of their fallen leader.

Chile had its reputation for stability well tested in 1910 when the executive changed four times without the slightest political disturbance. According to the constitution, the officer who takes the place of the President in case of the latter's death or disability, though vested with full authority, has the title of Vice President only. It so happened that after the death of the President two members of the Cabinet in succession held the vice presidency, and they were followed by the chief magistrate, who was duly elected and installed at the close of the year. In 1915, for the first time since their leader had committed suicide, one of the followers of Balmaceda was chosen President — by a strange coalition of Liberal-Democrats, or Balmacedists, Conservatives, and Nationalists, over the candidate of the Radicals, Liberals, and Democrats. The maintenance of the parliamentary system, however, continued to produce frequent alterations in the personnel of the Cabinet.

In its foreign relations, apart from the adjustment reached with Argentina, Chile managed to settle the difficulties with Bolivia arising out of the War of the Pacific. By the terms of treaties concluded in 1895 and 1905, the region tentatively transferred by the armistice of 1884 was ceded outright to Chile in return for a seaport and a narrow right of way to it through the former Peruvian province of Tarapacá. With Peru, Chile was not so fortunate. Though the tension over the ultimate disposal of the Tacna and Arica question was somewhat reduced, it was far from being removed. Chile absolutely refused to submit the matter to arbitration, on the ground that such a procedure could not properly be applied to a question arising out of a war that had taken place so many years before. Chile did not wish to give the region up, lest by so doing it might expose Tarapacá to a possible attack from Peru. The investment of large amounts of foreign capital in the exploitation of the deposits of nitrate of soda had made that province economically very valuable, and the export tax levied on the product was the chief source of the national revenue. These were all potent reasons why Chile wanted to keep its hold on Tacna and Arica. Besides, possession was nine points in the law!

On the other hand, the original plan of having the question decided by a vote of the inhabitants of the provinces concerned was not carried into effect, partly because both claimants cherished a conviction that whichever lost the election would deny its validity, and partly because they could not agree upon the precise method of holding it. Chile suggested that the international commission which was selected to take charge of the plebiscite, and which was composed of a Chilean, a Peruvian, and a neutral, should be presided over by the Chilean member as representative of the country actually in possession, whereas Peru insisted that the neutral should act as chairman. Chile proposed also that Chileans, Peruvians, and foreigners resident in the area six months before the date of the elections should vote, provided that they had the right to do so under the terms of the constitutions of both states. Peru, on its part, objected to the length of residence, and wished to limit carefully the number of Chilean voters, to exclude foreigners altogether from the election, and to disregard qualifications for the suffrage which required an ability to read and write. Both countries, moreover, appeared to have a lurking suspicion that in any event the other would try to secure a majority at the polls by supplying a requisite number of voters drawn from their respective citizenry who were not ordinarily resident in Tacna and Arica! Unable to overcome the deadlock, Chile and Peru agreed in 1913 to postpone the settlement for twenty years longer. At the expiration of this period, when Chile would have held the provinces for half a century, the question should be finally adjusted on bases mutually satisfactory. Officially amicable relations were then restored.

While the political situation in Bolivia remained stable, so much could not be said of that in Peru and Ecuador. If the troubles in the former were more or less military, a persistence of the conflict between clericals and radicals characterized the commotions in the latter, because of certain liberal provisions in the Constitution of 1907. Peru, on the other hand, in 1915 guaranteed its people the enjoyment of religious liberty.

Next to the Tacna and Arica question, the dubious boundaries of Ecuador constituted the most serious international problem in South America. The so-called Oriente region, lying east of the Andes and claimed by Peru, Brazil, and Colombia, appeared differently on different maps, according as one claimant nation or another set forth its own case. Had all three been satisfied, nothing would have been left of Ecuador but the strip between the Andes and the Pacific coast, including the cities of Quito and Guayaquil. The Ecuadorians, therefore, were bitterly sensitive on the subject.

Protracted negotiations over the boundaries became alike tedious and listless. But the moment that the respective diplomats had agreed upon some knotty point, the Congress of one litigant or another was almost sure to reject the decision and start the controversy all over again. Even reference of the matter to the arbitral judgment of European monarchs produced, so far as Ecuador and Peru were concerned, riotous attacks upon the Peruvian legation and consulates, charges and countercharges of invasion of each other's territory, and the suspension of diplomatic relations. Though the United States, Argentina, and Brazil had interposed to ward off an armed conflict between the two republics and, in 1911, had urged that the dispute be submitted to the Hague Tribunal, nothing would induce Ecuador to comply.

Colombia was even more unfortunate than its southern neighbor, for in addition to political convulsions it suffered financial disaster and an actual deprivation of territory. Struggles among factions, official influence at the elections, dictatorships, and fighting between the departments and the national Government plunged the country, in 1899, into the worst civil war it had known for many a day. Paper money, issued in unlimited amounts and given a forced circulation, made the distress still more acute. Then came the hardest blow of all. Since 1830 Panamá, as province or state, had tried many times to secede from Colombia. In 1903 the opportunity it sought became altogether favorable. The parent nation, just beginning to recover from the disasters of civil strife, would probably be unable to prevent a new attempt at withdrawal. The people of Panamá, of course, knew how eager the United States was to acquire the region of the proposed Canal Zone, since it had failed to win it by negotiation with Colombia. Accordingly, if they were to start a "revolution," they had reason to believe that it would not lack support — or at least, connivance — from that quarter.

On the 3d of November the projected "revolution" occurred, on schedule time, and the United States recognized the independence of the "Republic of Panamá" three days later! In return for a guarantee of independence, however, the United States stipulated, in the convention concluded on the 18th of November, that, besides authority to enforce sanitary regulations in the Canal Zone, it should also have the right of intervention to maintain order in the republic itself. More than once, indeed, after Panamá adopted its constitution in 1904, elections threatened to become tumultuous; whereupon the United States saw to it that they passed off quietly.

Having no wish to flout their huge neighbor to the northward, the Hispanic nations at large hastened to acknowledge the independence of the new republic, despite the indignation that prevailed in press and public over what was regarded as an act of despoilment. In view of the resentful attitude of Colombia and mindful also of the opinion of many Americans that a gross injustice had been committed, the United States eventually offered terms of settlement. It agreed to express regret for the ill feeling between the two countries which had arisen out of the Panamá incident, provided that such expression were made mutual; and, as a species of indemnity, it agreed to pay for canal rights to be acquired in Colombian territory and for the lease of certain islands as naval stations. But neither the terms nor the amount of the compensation proved acceptable. Instead, Colombia urged that the whole matter be referred to the judgment of the tribunal at The Hague.

Alluding to the use made of the liberties won in the struggle for emancipation from Spain by the native land of Miranda, Bolívar, and Sucre, on the part of the country which had been in the vanguard of the fight for freedom from a foreign yoke, a writer of Venezuela once declared that it had not elected legally a single President; had not put democratic ideas or institutions into practice; had lived wholly under dictatorships; had neglected public instruction; and had set up a large number of oppressive commercial monopolies, including the navigation of rivers, the coastwise trade, the pearl fisheries, and the sale of tobacco, salt, sugar, liquor, matches, explosives, butter, grease, cement, shoes, meat, and flour. Exaggerated as the indictment is and applicable also, though in less degree, to some of the other backward countries of Hispanic America, it contains unfortunately a large measure of truth. Indeed, so far as Venezuela itself is concerned, this critic might have added that every time a "restorer," "regenerator," or "liberator" succumbed there, the old craze for federalism again broke out and menaced the nation with piecemeal destruction. Obedient, furthermore, to the whims of a presidential despot, Venezuela perpetrated more outrages on foreigners and created more international friction after 1899 than any other land in Spanish America had ever done.

While the formidable Guzmán Blanco was still alive, the various Presidents acted cautiously. No sooner had he passed away than disorder broke out afresh. Since a new dictator thought he needed a longer term of office and divers other administrative advantages, a constitution incorporating them was framed and published in the due and customary manner. This had hardly gone into operation when, in 1895, a contest arose with Great Britain about the boundaries between Venezuela and British Guiana. Under pressure from the United States, however, the matter was referred to arbitration, and Venezuela came out substantially the loser.

In 1899 there appeared on the scene a personage compared with whom Zelaya was the merest novice in the art of making trouble. This was Cipriano Castro, the greatest international nuisance of the early twentieth century. A rude, arrogant, fearless, energetic, capricious mountaineer and cattleman, he regarded foreigners no less than his own countryfolk, it would seem, as objects for his particular scorn, displeasure, exploitation, or amusement, as the case might be. He was greatly angered by the way in which foreigners in dispute with local officials avoided a resort to Venezuelan courts and — still worse — rejected their decisions and appealed instead to their diplomatic representatives for protection. He declared such a procedure to be an affront to the national dignity. Yet foreigners were usually correct in affirming that judges appointed by an arbitrary President were little more than figureheads, incapable of dispensing justice, even were they so inclined.

Jealous not only of his personal prestige but of what he imagined, or pretended to imagine, were the rights of a small nation, Castro tried throughout to portray the situation in such a light as to induce the other Hispanic republics also to view foreign interference as a dire peril to their own independence and sovereignty; and he further endeavored to involve the United States in a struggle with European powers as a means possibly of testing the efficacy of the Monroe Doctrine or of laying bare before the world the evil nature of American imperialistic designs.

By the year 1901, in which Venezuela adopted another constitution, the revolutionary disturbances had materially diminished the revenues from the customs. Furthermore Castro's regulations exacting military service of all males between fourteen and sixty years of age had filled the prisons to overflowing. Many foreigners who had suffered in consequence resorted to measures of self-defense — among them representatives of certain American and British asphalt companies which were working concessions granted by Castro's predecessors. Though familiar with what commonly happens to those who handle pitch, they had not scrupled to aid some of Castro's enemies. Castro forthwith imposed on them enormous fines which amounted practically to a confiscation of their rights.

While the United States and Great Britain were expostulating over this behavior of the despot,

France broke off diplomatic relations with Venezuela because of Castro's refusal either to pay or to submit to arbitration certain claims which had originated in previous revolutions. Germany, aggrieved in similar fashion, contemplated a seizure of the customs until its demands for redress were satisfied. And then came Italy with like causes of complaint. As if these complications were not sufficient, Venezuela came to blows with Colombia.

As the foreign pressure on Castro steadily increased, Luís María Drago, the Argentine Minister of Foreign Affairs, formulated in 1902 the doctrine with which his name has been associated. It stated in substance that force should never be employed between nations for the collection of contractual debts. Encouraged by this apparent token of support from a sister republic, Castro defied his array of foreign adversaries more vigorously than ever, declaring that he might find it needful to invade the United States, by way of New Orleans, to teach it the lesson it deserved! But when he attempted, in the following year, to close the ports of Venezuela as a means of bringing his native antagonists to terms, Great Britain, Germany, and Italy seized his warships, blockaded the coast, and bombarded some of his forts. Thereupon the United

States interposed with a suggestion that the dispute be laid before the Hague Tribunal. Although Castro yielded, he did not fail to have a clause inserted in a new "constitution" requiring foreigners who might wish to enter the republic to show certificates of good character from the Governments of their respective countries.

These incidents gave much food for thought to Castro as well as to his soberer compatriots. The European powers had displayed an apparent willingness to have the United States, if it chose to do so, assume the rôle of a New World policeman and financial guarantor. Were it to assume these duties, backward republics in the Caribbean and its vicinity were likely to have their affairs, internal as well as external, supervised by the big nation in order to ward off European intervention. At this moment, indeed, the United States was intervening in Panamá. The prospect aroused in many Hispanic countries the fear of a "Yankee peril" greater even than that emanating from Europe. Instead of being a kindly and disinterested protector of small neighbors, the "Colossus of the North" appeared rather to resemble a political and commercial ogre bent upon swallowing them to satisfy "manifest destiny."

Having succeeded in putting around his head an aureole of local popularity, Castro in 1905 picked a new set of partially justified quarrels with the United States, Great Britain, France, Italy, Colombia, and even with the Netherlands, arising out of the depredations of revolutionists; but an armed menace from the United States induced him to desist from his plans. He contented himself accordingly with issuing a decree of amnesty for all political offenders except the leaders. When "re-elected," he carried his magnanimity so far as to resign awhile in favor of the Vice President, stating that, if his retirement were to bring peace and concord, he would make it permanent. But as he saw to it that his temporary withdrawal should not have this happy result, he came back again to his former position a few months later.

Venting his wrath upon the Netherlands because its minister had reported to his Government an outbreak of cholera at La Guaira, the chief seaport of Venezuela, the dictator laid an embargo on Dutch commerce, seized its ships, and denounced the Dutch for their alleged failure to check filibustering from their islands off the coast. When the minister protested, Castro expelled him. Thereupon the Netherlands instituted a blockade of the Venezuelan ports.

What might have happened if Castro had remained much longer in charge, may be guessed. Toward the close of 1908, however, he departed for Europe to undergo a course of medical treatment. Hardly had he left Venezuelan shores when Juan Vicente Gómez, the able, astute, and vigorous Vice President, managed to secure his own election to the presidency and an immediate recognition from foreign states. Under his direction all of the international tangles of Venezuela were straightened out.

In 1914 the country adopted its eleventh constitution and thereby lengthened the presidential term to seven years, shortened that of members of the lower house of the Congress to four, determined definitely the number of States in the union, altered the apportionment of their congressional representation, and enlarged the powers of the federal Government — or, rather, those of its executive branch! In 1914 Gómez resigned office in favor of the Vice President, and secured an appointment instead as commander in chief of the army. This procedure was promptly denounced as a trick to evade the constitutional prohibition of two consecutive terms. A year later he was unanimously elected President, though he never formally took the oath of office.

Whatever may be thought of the political ways and means of this new Guzmán Blanco to maintain himself as a power behind or on the presidential throne, Gómez gave Venezuela an administration of a sort very different from that of his immediate predecessor. He suppressed various government monopolies, removed other obstacles to the material advancement of the country, and reduced the national debt. He did much also to improve the sanitary conditions at La Guaira, and he promoted education, especially the teaching of foreign languages.

Gómez nevertheless had to keep a watchful eye on the partisans of Castro, who broke out in revolt whenever they had an opportunity. The United States, Great Britain, France, the Netherlands, Denmark, Cuba, and Colombia eyed the movements of the ex-dictator nervously, as European powers long ago were wont to do in the case of a certain Man of Destiny, and barred him out of both their possessions and Venezuela itself. International patience, never Job-like, had been too sorely vexed to permit his return. Nevertheless, after the manner of the ancient persecutor of the Biblical martyr, Castro did not refrain from going to and fro in the earth. In fact he still "walketh about" seeking to recover his hold upon Venezuela!

CHAPTER X

MEXICO IN REVOLUTION

When, in 1910, like several of its sister republics, Mexico celebrated the centennial anniversary of its independence, the era of peace and progress inaugurated by Porfirio Díaz seemed likely to last indefinitely, for he was entering upon his eighth term as President. Brilliant as his career had been, however, and greatly as Mexico had prospered under his rigid rule, a sullen discontent had been brewing. The country that had had but one continuous President in twenty-six years was destined to have some fourteen chief magistrates in less than a quarter of that time, and to surpass all its previous records for rapidity in presidential succession, by having one executive who is said to have held office for precisely fifty-six minutes!

It has often been asserted that the reason for the downfall of Díaz and the lapse of Mexico into the unhappy conditions of a half century earlier was that he had grown too old to keep a firm grip on the situation. It has also been declared that his insistence upon reëlection and upon the elevation of his own personal candidate to the vice presidency, as a successor in case of his retirement, occasioned his overthrow. The truth of the matter is that these circumstances were only incidental to his downfall; the real causes of revolution lay deep-rooted in the history of these twenty-six years. The most significant feature of the revolt was its civilian character. A widespread public opinion had been created; a national consciousness had been awakened which was intolerant of abuses and determined upon their removal at any cost; and this public opinion and national consciousness were products of general education, which had brought to the fore a number of intelligent men eager to participate in public affairs and yet barred out because of their unwillingness to support the existing régime.

Some one has remarked, and rightly, that Díaz in his zeal for the material advancement of Mexico, mistook the tangible wealth of the country for its welfare. Desirable and even necessary as that material progress was, it produced only a one-sided prosperity. Díaz was singularly deaf to the just complaints of the people of the laboring classes, who, as manufacturing and other industrial enterprises developed, were resolved to better their conditions. In the country at large the discontent was still stronger. Throughout many of the rural districts general advancement had been retarded because of the holding of huge areas of fertile land by a comparatively few rich families, who did little to improve it and were content with small returns from the labor of throngs of unskilled native cultivators. Wretchedly paid and housed, and toiling long hours, the workers lived like the serfs of medieval days or as their own ancestors did in colonial times. Ignorant, poverty-stricken, liable at any moment to be dispossessed of the tiny patch of ground on which they raised a few hills of corn or beans, most of them were naturally a simple, peaceful folk who, in spite of their misfortunes, might have gone on indefinitely with their drudgery in a hopeless apathetic fashion, unless their latent savage instincts happened to be aroused by drink and the prospect of plunder. On the other hand, the intelligent among them, knowing that in some of the northern States of the republic wages were higher and treatment fairer, felt a sense of wrong which, like that of the laboring class in the towns, was all the more dangerous because it was not allowed to find expression.

Díaz thought that what Mexico required above everything else was the development of industrial efficiency and financial strength, assured by a maintenance of absolute order. Though disposed to do justice in individual cases, he would tolerate no class movements of any kind. Labor unions, strikes, and other efforts at lightening the burden of the workers he regarded as seditious and deserving of severe punishment. In order to attract capital from abroad as the best means of exploiting the vast resources of the country, he was willing to go to any length, it would seem, in guaranteeing protection. Small wonder, therefore, that the people who shared in none of the immediate advantages from that source should have muttered that Mexico was the "mother of foreigners and the stepmother of Mexicans." And, since so much of the capital came from the United States, the antiforeign sentiment singled Americans out for its particular dislike.

If Díaz appeared unable to appreciate the significance of the educational and industrial awakening, he was no less oblivious of the political outcome. He knew, of course, that the Mexican constitution made impossible demands upon the political capacity of the people. He was himself mainly of Indian blood and he believed that he understood the temperament and limitations of most Mexicans. Knowing how tenaciously they clung to political notions, he believed that it was safer and wiser to forego, at least for a time, real popular government and to concentrate power in the hands of a strong man who could maintain order.

Accordingly, backed by his political adherents, known as *científicos* (doctrinaires), some of whom had acquired a sinister ascendancy over him, and also by the Church, the landed proprietors, and the foreign capitalists, Díaz centered the entire administration more and more in himself. Elections became mere farces. Not only the federal officials themselves but the state governors, the members of the state legislatures, and all others in authority during the later years of his rule owed their selection primarily to him and held their positions only if personally loyal to him. Confident of his support and certain that protests against misgovernment would be regarded by the President as seditious, many of them abused their power at will. Notable among them were the local officials, called *jefes políticos*, whose control of the police force enabled them to indulge in practices of intimidation and extortion which ultimately became unendurable.

Though symptoms of popular wrath against the Díaz régime, or *diazpotism* as the Mexicans termed it, were apparent as early as 1908, it was not until January, 1911, that the actual revolution came. It was headed by Francisco I. Madero, a member of a wealthy and distinguished family of landed proprietors in one of the northern States. What the revolutionists demanded in substance was the retirement of the President, Vice President, and Cabinet; a return to the principle of no reëlection to the chief magistracy; a guarantee of fair elections at all times; the choice of capable, honest, and impartial judges, *jefes políticos*, and other officials; and, in particular, a series of agrarian and industrial reforms which would break up the great estates, create peasant proprietorships, and better the conditions of the working classes. Disposed at first to treat the insurrection lightly, Díaz soon found that he had underestimated its strength. Grants of some of the demands and promises of reform were met with a dogged insistence upon his own resignation. Then, as the rebellion spread to the southward, the masterful old man realized that his thirty-one years of rule were at an end. On the 25th of May, therefore, he gave up his power and sailed for Europe.

Madero was chosen President five months later, but the revolution soon passed beyond his control. He was a sincere idealist, if not something of a visionary, actuated by humane and kindly sentiments, but he lacked resoluteness and the art of managing men. He was too prolific, also, of promises which he must have known he could not keep. Yielding to family influence, he let his followers get out of hand. Ambitious chieftains and groups of Radicals blocked and thwarted him at every turn. When he could find no means of carrying out his program without wholesale confiscation and the disruption of business interests, he was accused of abandoning his duty. One officer after another deserted him and turned rebel. Brigandage and insurrection swept over the country and threatened to involve it in ugly complications with the United States and European powers. At length, in February, 1913, came the blow that put an end to all of Madero's efforts and aspirations. A military uprising in the city of Mexico made him prisoner, forced him to resign, and set up a provisional government under the dictatorship of Victoriano Huerta, one of his chief lieutenants. Two weeks later both Madero and the Vice President were assassinated while on their way supposedly to a place of safety.

Huerta was a rough soldier of Indian origin, possessed of unusual force of character and strength of will, ruthless, cunning, and in bearing alternately dignified and vulgar. A *científico* in political faith, he was disposed to restore the Díaz régime, so far as an application of shrewdness and force could make it possible. But from the outset he found an obstacle confronting him that he could not surmount. Though acknowledged by European countries and by many of the Hispanic republics, he could not win recognition from the United States, either as provisional President or as a candidate for regular election to the office. Whether personally responsible for the murder of Madero or not, he was not regarded by the American Government as entitled to recognition, on the ground that he was not the choice of the Mexican people. In its refusal to recognize an administration set up merely by brute force, the United States was upheld by Argentina, Brazil, Chile, and Cuba. The elimination of Huerta became the chief feature for a while of its Mexican policy.

Meanwhile the followers of Madero and the

pronounced Radicals had found a new northern leader in the person of Venustiano Carranza. They called themselves Constitutionalists, as indicative of their purpose to reëstablish the constitution and to choose a successor to Madero in a constitutional manner. What they really desired was those radical changes along social, industrial, and political lines, which Madero had championed in theory. They sought to introduce a species of socialistic régime that would provide the Mexicans with an opportunity for self-regeneration. While Díaz had believed in economic progress supported by the great landed proprietors, the moral influence of the Church, and the application of foreign capital, the Constitutionalists, personified in Carranza, were convinced that these agencies, if left free and undisturbed to work their will, would ruin Mexico. Though not exactly antiforeign in their attitude, they wished to curb the power of the foreigner; they would accept his aid whenever desirable for the economic development of the country, but they would not submit to his virtual control of public affairs. In any case they would tolerate no interference by the United States. Compromise with the Huerta régime, therefore, was impossible. Huerta, the "strong man" of the Díaz type, must go. On this point, at least, the Constitutionalists were in thorough agreement with the United States.

A variety of international complications ensued. Both Huertistas and Carranzistas perpetrated outrages on foreigners, which evoked sharp protests and threats from the United States and European powers. While careful not to recognize his opponents officially, the American Government resorted to all kinds of means to oust the dictator. An embargo was laid on the export of arms and munitions; all efforts to procure financial help from abroad were balked. The power of Huerta was waning perceptibly and that of the Constitutionalists was increasing when an incident that occurred in April, 1914, at Tampico brought matters to a climax. A number of American sailors who had gone ashore to obtain supplies were arrested and temporarily detained. The United States demanded that the American flag be saluted as reparation for the insult. Upon the refusal of Huerta to comply, the United States sent a naval expedition to occupy Vera Cruz.

Both Carranza and Huerta regarded this move as equivalent to an act of war. Argentina, Brazil, and Chile then offered their mediation. But the conference arranged for this purpose at Niagara

Falls, Canada, had before it a task altogether impossible of accomplishment. Though Carranza was willing to have the Constitutionalists represented, if the discussion related solely to the immediate issue between the United States and Huerta, he declined to extend the scope of the conference so as to admit the right of the United States to interfere in the internal affairs of Mexico. The conference accomplished nothing so far as the immediate issue was concerned. The dictator did not make reparation for the "affronts and indignities" he had committed; but his day was over. The advance of the Constitutionalists southward compelled him in July to abandon the capital and leave the country. Four months later the American forces were withdrawn from Vera Cruz. The "A B C" Conference, however barren it was of direct results, helped to allay suspicions of the United States in Hispanic America and brought appreciably nearer a "concert of the western world."

While far from exercising full control throughout Mexico, the "first chief" of the Constitutionalists was easily the dominant figure in the situation. At home a ranchman, in public affairs a statesman of considerable ability, knowing how to insist and yet how to temporize, Carranza carried on a struggle, both in arms and in diplomacy, which singled him out as a remarkable character. Shrewdly aware of the advantageous circumstances afforded him by the war in Europe, he turned them to account with a degree of skill that blocked every attempt at defeat or compromise. No matter how serious the opposition to him in Mexico itself, how menacing the attitude of the United States, or how persuasive the conciliatory disposition of Hispanic American nations, he clung stubbornly and tenaciously to his program.

Even after Huerta had been eliminated, Carranza's position was not assured, for Francisco, or "Pancho," Villa, a chieftain whose personal qualities resembled those of the fallen dictator, was equally determined to eliminate him. For a brief moment, indeed, peace reigned. Under an alleged agreement between them, a convention of Constitutionalist officers was to choose a provisional President, who should be ineligible as a candidate for the permanent presidency at the regular elections. When Carranza assumed both of these positions, Villa declared his act a violation of their understanding and insisted upon his retirement. Inasmuch as the convention was dominated by Villa, the "first chief" decided to ignore its election of a provisional President.

The struggle between the Conventionalists headed by Villa and the Constitutionalists under Carranza plunged Mexico into worse discord and misery than ever. Indeed it became a sort of three-cornered contest. The third party was Emiliano Zapata, an Indian bandit, nominally a supporter of Villa but actually favorable to neither of the rivals. Operating near the capital, he plundered Conventionalists and Constitutionalists with equal impartiality, and as a diversion occasionally occupied the city itself. These circumstances gave force to the saying that Mexico was a "land where peace breaks out once in a while!"

Early in 1915 Carranza proceeded to issue a number of radical decrees that exasperated foreigners almost beyond endurance. Rather than resort to extreme measures again, however, the United States invoked the coöperation of the Hispanic republics and proposed a conference to devise some solution of the Mexican problem. To give the proposed conference a wider representation, it invited not only the "A B C" powers, but Bolivia, Uruguay, and Guatemala to participate. Meeting at Washington in August, the mediators encountered the same difficulty which had confronted their predecessors at Niagara Falls. Though the other chieftains assented, Carranza, now certain of success, declined to heed any proposal of conciliation. Characterizing efforts of the kind as an unwarranted interference in the internal affairs of a sister nation, he warned the Hispanic republics against setting up so dangerous a precedent. In reply Argentina stated that the conference obeyed a "lofty inspiration of Pan-American solidarity, and, instead of finding any cause for alarm, the Mexican people should see in it a proof of their friendly consideration that her fate evokes in us, and calls forth our good wishes for her pacification and development." However, as the only apparent escape from more watchful waiting or from armed intervention on the part of the United States, in October the seven Governments decided to accept the facts as they stood, and accordingly recognized Carranza as the *de facto* ruler of Mexico.

Enraged at this favor shown to his rival, Villa determined deliberately to provoke American intervention by a murderous raid on a town in New Mexico in March, 1916. When the United States dispatched an expedition to avenge the outrage, Carranza protested energetically against its violation of Mexican territory and demanded its withdrawal. Several clashes, in fact, occurred between American soldiers and Carranzistas. Neither the expedition itself, however, nor diplomatic efforts to find some method of coöperation which would prevent constant trouble along the frontier served any useful purpose, since Villa apparently could not be captured and Carranza refused to yield to diplomatic persuasion. Carranza then proposed that a joint commission be appointed to settle these vexed questions. Even this device proved wholly unsatisfactory. The Mexicans would not concede the right of the United States to send an armed expedition into their country at any time, and the Americans refused to accept limitations on the kind of troops that they might employ or on the zone of their operations. In January, 1917, the joint commission was dissolved and the American soldiers were withdrawn. Again the "first chief" had won!

On the 5th of February a convention assembled at Querétaro promulgated a constitution embodying substantially all of the radical program that Carranza had anticipated in his decrees. Besides providing for an elaborate improvement in the condition of the laboring classes and for such a division of great estates as might satisfy their particular needs, the new constitution imposed drastic restrictions upon foreigners and religious bodies. Under its terms, foreigners could not acquire industrial concessions unless they waived their treaty rights and consented to regard themselves for the purpose as Mexican citizens. In all such cases preference was to be shown Mexicans over foreigners. Ecclesiastical corporations were forbidden to own real property. No primary school and no charitable institution could be conducted by any religious mission or denomination, and religious publications must refrain from commenting on public affairs. The presidential term was reduced from six years to four; reëlection was prohibited; and the office of Vice President was abolished.

When, on the 1st of May, Venustiano Carranza was chosen President, Mexico had its first constitutional executive in four years. After a cruel and obstinately intolerant struggle that had occasioned indescribable suffering from disease and starvation, as well as the usual slaughter and destruction incident to war, the country began to enjoy once more a measure of peace. Financial exhaustion, however, had to be overcome before recuperation was possible. Industrial progress had become almost paralyzed; vast quantities of depreciated paper money had to be withdrawn from circulation; and an enormous array of claims for the loss of foreign life and property had rolled up.

CHAPTER XI

THE REPUBLICS OF THE CARIBBEAN

The course of events in certain of the republics in and around the Caribbean Sea warned the Hispanic nations that independence was a relative condition and that it might vary in direct ratio with nearness to the United States. After 1906 this powerful northern neighbor showed an unmistakable tendency to extend its influence in various ways. Here fiscal and police control was established; there official recognition was withheld from a President who had secured office by unconstitutional methods. Nonrecognition promised to be an effective way of maintaining a régime of law and order, as the United States understood those terms. Assurances from the United States of the full political equality of all republics, big or little, in the western hemisphere did not always carry conviction to Spanish American ears. The smaller countries in and around the Caribbean

Sea, at least, seemed likely to become virtually American protectorates.

Like their Hispanic neighbor on the north, the little republics of Central America were also scenes of political disturbance. None of them except Panamá escaped revolutionary uprisings, though the loss of life and property was insignificant. On the other hand, in these early years of the century the five countries north of Panamá made substantial progress toward federation. As a South American writer has expressed it, their previous efforts in that direction "amid sumptuous festivals, banquets and other solemn public acts" at which they "intoned in lyric accents daily hymns for the imperishable reunion of the isthmian republics," had been as illusory as they were frequent.

Despite the mediation of the United States and Mexico in 1906, while the latter was still ruled by Díaz, the struggle in which Nicaragua, Honduras, Guatemala, and Salvador had been engaged was soon renewed between the first two belligerents. Since diplomatic interposition no longer availed, American marines were landed in Nicaragua, and the bumptious Zelaya was induced to have his country meet its neighbors in a conference at Washington. Under the auspices of the United

States and Mexico, in December, 1907, representatives of the five republics signed a series of conventions providing for peace and coöperation. An arbitral court of justice, to be erected in Costa Rica and composed of one judge from each nation, was to decide all matters of dispute which could not be adjusted through ordinary diplomatic means. Here, also, an institute for the training of Central American teachers was to be established. Annual conferences were to discuss, and an office in Guatemala was to record, measures designed to secure uniformity in financial, commercial, industrial, sanitary, and educational regulations. Honduras, the storm center of weakness, was to be neutralized. None of the States was thereafter to recognize in any of them a government which had been set up in an illegal fashion. A "Constitutional Act of Central American Fraternity," moreover, was adopted on behalf of peace, harmony, and progress. Toward a realization of the several objects of the conference, the Presidents of the five republics were to invite their colleagues of the United States and Mexico, whenever needful, to appoint representatives, to "lend their good offices in a purely friendly way."

Though most of these agencies were promptly

put into operation, the results were not altogether satisfactory. Some discords, to be sure, were removed by treaties settling boundary questions and providing for reciprocal trade advantages; but it is doubtful whether the arrangements devised at Washington would have worked at all if the United States had not kept the little countries under a certain amount of observation. What the Central Americans apparently preferred was to be left alone, some of them to mind their own business, others to mind their neighbor's affairs.

Of all the Central American countries Honduras was, perhaps, the one most afflicted with pecuniary misfortunes. In 1909 its foreign debt, along with arrears of interest unpaid for thirty-seven years, was estimated at upwards of $110,000,000. Of this amount a large part consisted of loans obtained from foreign capitalists, at more or less extortionate rates, for the construction of a short railway, of which less than half had been built. That revolutions should be rather chronic in a land where so much money could be squandered and where the temperaments of Presidents and ex-Presidents were so bellicose, was natural enough. When the United States could not induce the warring rivals to abide by fair elections, it sent a force of marines to overawe them and gave warning that further disturbances would not be allowed.

In Nicaragua the conditions were similar. Here Zelaya, restive under the limitations set by the conference at Washington, yearned to become the "strong man" of Central America, who would teach the Yankees to stop their meddling. But his downfall was imminent. In 1909, as the result of his execution of two American soldiers of fortune who had taken part in a recent insurrection, the United States resolved to tolerate Zelaya no longer. Openly recognizing the insurgents, it forced the dictator out of the country. Three years later, when a President-elect started to assume office before the legally appointed time, a force of American marines at the capital convinced him that such a procedure was undesirable. The "corrupt and barbarous" conditions prevailing in Zelaya's time, he was informed, could not be tolerated. The United States, in fact, notified all parties in Nicaragua that, under the terms of the Washington conventions, it had a "moral mandate to exert its influence for the preservation of the general peace of Central America." Since those agreements had vested no one with authority to enforce them, such an interpretation of their language, aimed apparently at all disturbances, foreign as well as domestic, was rather elastic! At all events, after 1912, when a new constitution was adopted, the country became relatively quiet and somewhat progressive. Whenever a political flurry did take place, American marines were employed to preserve the peace. Many citizens, therefore, declined to vote, on the ground that the moral and material support thus furnished by the great nation to the northward rendered it futile for them to assume political responsibilities.

Meanwhile negotiations began which were ultimately to make Nicaragua a fiscal protectorate of the United States. American officials were chosen to act as financial advisers and collectors of customs, and favorable arrangements were concluded with American bankers regarding the monetary situation; but it was not until 1916 that a treaty covering this situation was ratified. According to its provisions, in return for a stipulated sum to be expended under American direction, Nicaragua was to grant to the United States the exclusive privilege of constructing a canal through the territory of the republic and to lease to it the Corn Islands and a part of Fonseca Bay, on the Pacific coast, for use as naval stations. The prospect of American intervention alarmed the neighboring republics. Asserting that the treaty infringed upon their respective boundaries, Costa Rica and Salvador brought suit against Nicaragua before the Central American Court. With the exception of the Nicaraguan representative, the judges upheld the contention of the plaintiffs that the defendant had no right to make any such concessions without previous consultation with Costa Rica, Salvador, and Honduras, since all three alike were affected by them. The Court observed, however, that it could not declare the treaty void because the United States, one of the parties concerned, was not subject to its jurisdiction. Nicaragua declined to accept the decision; and the United States, the country responsible for the existence of the Court and presumably interested in helping to enforce its judgment, allowed it to go out of existence in 1918 on the expiration of its ten-year term.

The economic situation of Costa Rica brought about a state of affairs wholly unusual in Central American politics. The President, Alfredo González, wished to reform the system of taxation so that a fairer share of the public burdens should fall on the great landholders who, like most of their brethren in the Hispanic countries, were practically exempt. This project, coupled with the fact that certain American citizens seeking an oil concession had undermined the power of the President by wholesale bribery, induced the Minister of War, in 1917, to start a revolt against him. Rather than shed the blood of his fellow citizens for mere personal advantages, González sustained the good reputation of Costa Rica for freedom from civil commotions by quietly leaving the country and going to the United States to present his case. In consequence, the American Government declined to recognize the *de facto* ruler.

Police and fiscal supervision by the United States has characterized the recent history of Panamá. Not only has a proposed increase in the customs duties been disallowed, but more than once the unrest attending presidential elections has required the calming presence of American officials. As a means of forestalling outbreaks, particularly in view of the cosmopolitan population resident on the Isthmus, the republic enacted a law in 1914 which forbade foreigners to mix in local politics and authorized the expulsion of naturalized citizens who attacked the Government through the press or otherwise. With the approval of the United States, Panamá entered into an agreement with American financiers providing for the creation of a national bank, one-fourth of the directors of which should be named by the Government of the republic.

The second period of American rule in Cuba lasted till 1909. Control of the Government was then formally transferred to José Miguel Gómez, the President who had been chosen by the Liberals at the elections held in the previous year; but the United States did not cease to watch over its chief Caribbean ward. A bitter controversy soon developed in the Cuban Congress over measures to forbid the further purchase of land by aliens, and to insure that a certain percentage of the public offices should be held by colored citizens. Though both projects were defeated, they revealed a strong antiforeign sentiment and much dissatisfaction on the part of the negro population. It was clear also that Gómez intended to oust all conservatives from office, for an obedient Congress passed a bill suspending the civil service rules.

The partisanship of Gómez and his supporters, together with the constant interference of military veterans in political affairs, provoked numerous outbreaks, which led the United States, in 1912, to warn Cuba that it might again be compelled to intervene. Eventually, when a negro insurrection in the eastern part of the island menaced the safety of foreigners, American marines were landed. Another instance of intervention was the objection by the United States to an employers' liability law that would have given a monopoly of the insurance business to a Cuban company to the detriment of American firms.

After the election of Mario Menocal, the Conservative candidate, to the presidency in 1912, another occasion for intervention presented itself. An amnesty bill, originally drafted for the purpose of freeing the colored insurgents and other offenders, was amended so as to empower the retiring President to grant pardon before trial to persons whom his successor wished to prosecute for wholesale corruption in financial transactions. Before the bill passed, however, notice was sent from Washington that, since the American Government had the authority to supervise the finances of the republic, Gómez would better veto the bill, and this he accordingly did.

A sharp struggle arose when it became known that Menocal would be a candidate for reëlection. The Liberal majority in the Congress passed a bill requiring that a President who sought to succeed himself should resign two months before the elections. When Menocal vetoed this measure, his opponents demanded that the United States supervise the elections. As the result of the elections was doubtful, Gómez and his followers resorted in 1917 to the usual insurrection; whereupon the American Government warned the rebels that it would not recognize their claims if they won by force. Active aid from that quarter, as well as the capture of the insurgent leader, caused the movement to collapse after the electoral college had decided in favor of Menocal.

In the Dominican Republic disturbances were frequent, notwithstanding the fact that American officials were in charge of the customhouses and by their presence were expected to exert a quieting influence. Even the adoption, in 1908, of a new constitution which provided for the prolongation of the presidential term to six years and for the abolition of the office of Vice President — two stabilizing devices quite common in Hispanic countries where personal ambition is prone to be a source of political trouble — did not help much to restore order. The assassination of the President and the persistence of age-long quarrels with Haiti over boundaries made matters worse.

Thereupon, in 1913, the United States served formal notice on the rebellious parties that it would not only refuse to recognize any Government set up by force but would withhold any share in the receipts from the customs. As this procedure did not prevent a revolutionary leader from demanding half a million dollars as a financial sedative for his political nerves and from creating more trouble when the President failed to dispense it, the heavy hand of an American naval force administered another kind of specific, until commissioners from Porto Rico could arrive to superintend the selection of a new chief magistrate. Notwithstanding the protest of the Dominican Government, the "fairest and freest" elections ever known in the country were held under the direction of those officials — as a "body of friendly observers"!

However amicable this arrangement seemed, it did not smother the flames of discord. In 1916, when an American naval commander suggested that a rebellious Minister of War leave the capital, he agreed to do so if the "fairest and freest" of chosen Presidents would resign. Even after both of them had complied with the suggestions, the individuals who assumed their respective offices were soon at loggerheads. Accordingly the United States placed the republic under military rule, until a President could be elected who might be able to retain his post without too much "friendly observation" from Washington, and a Minister of War could be appointed who would refrain from making war on the President! Then the organization of a new party to combat the previous inordinate display of personalities in politics created some hope that the republic would accomplish its own redemption.

Only because of its relation to the wars of emancipation and to the Dominican Republic, need the negro state of Haiti, occupying the western part of the Caribbean island, be mentioned in connection with the story of the Hispanic nations. Suffice it to say that the fact that their color was different and that they spoke a variant of French instead of Spanish did not prevent the inhabitants of this state from offering a far worse spectacle of political and financial demoralization than did their neighbors to the eastward. Perpetual commotions and repeated interventions by American and European naval forces on behalf of the foreign residents, eventually made it imperative for the United States to take direct charge of the republic. In 1916, by a convention which placed the finances under American control, created a native constabulary under American officers, and imposed a number of other restraints, the United States converted Haiti into what is practically a protectorate.

CHAPTER XII

PAN-AMERICANISM AND THE GREAT WAR

WHILE the Hispanic republics were entering upon the second century of their independent life, the idea of a certain community of interests between themselves and the United States began to assume a fairly definite form. Though emphasized by American statesmen and publicists in particular, the new point of view was not generally understood or appreciated by the people of either this country or its fellow nations to the southward. It seemed, nevertheless, to promise an effective coöperation in spirit and action between them and came therefore to be called "Pan-Americanism."

This sentiment of inter-American solidarity sprang from several sources. The periodical conferences of the United States and its sister republics gave occasion for an interchange of official courtesies and expressions of good feeling. Doubtless, also, the presence of delegates from the

Hispanic countries at the international gatherings at The Hague served to acquaint the world at large with the stability, strength, wealth, and culture of their respective lands. Individual Americans took an active interest in their fellows of Hispanic stock and found their interest reciprocated. Motives of business or pleasure and a desire to obtain personal knowledge about one another led to visits and countervisits that became steadily more frequent. Societies were created to encourage the friendship and acquaintance thus formed. Scientific congresses were held and institutes were founded in which both the United States and Hispanic America were represented. Books, articles, and newspaper accounts about one another's countries were published in increasing volume. Educational institutions devoted a constantly growing attention to inter-American affairs. Individuals and commissions were dispatched by the Hispanic nations and the United States to study one another's conditions and to confer about matters of mutual concern. Secretaries of State, Ministers of Foreign Affairs, and other distinguished personages interchanged visits. Above all, the common dangers and responsibilities falling upon the Americas at large as a consequence of the European war seemed likely to bring the several nations into a harmony of feeling and relationship to which they had never before attained.

Pan-Americanism, however, was destined to remain largely a generous ideal. The action of the United States in extending its direct influence over the small republics in and around the Caribbean aroused the suspicion and alarm of Hispanic Americans, who still feared imperialistic designs on the part of that country now more than ever the Colossus of the North. "The art of oratory among the Yankees," declared a South American critic, "is lavish with a fraternal idealism; but strong wills enforce their imperialistic ambitions." Impassioned speakers and writers adjured the ghost of Hispanic confederation to rise and confront the new northern peril. They even advocated an appeal to Great Britain, Germany, or Japan, and they urged closer economic, social, and intellectual relations with the countries of Europe.

It was while the United States was thus widening the sphere of its influence in the Caribbean that the "A B C" powers — Argentina, Brazil, and Chile — reached an understanding which was in a sense a measure of self-defense. For some years cordial relations had existed among these three nations which had grown so remarkably in strength and prestige. It was felt that by united action they might set up in the New World the European principle of a balance of power, assume the leadership in Hispanic America, and serve in some degree as a counterpoise to the United States. Nevertheless they were disposed to coöperate with their northern neighbor in the peaceable adjustment of conflicts in which other Hispanic countries were concerned, provided that the mediation carried on by such a "concert of the western world" did not include actual intervention in the internal affairs of the countries involved.

With this attitude of the public mind, it is not strange that the Hispanic republics at large should have been inclined to look with scant favor upon proposals made by the United States, in 1916, to render the spirit of Pan-Americanism more precise in its operation. The proposals in substance were these: that all the nations of America "mutually agree to guarantee the territorial integrity" of one another; to "maintain a republican form of government"; to prohibit the "exportation of arms to any but the legally constituted governments"; and to adopt laws of neutrality which would make it "impossible to filibustering expeditions to threaten or carry on revolutions in neighboring republics." These proposals appear to have received no formal approval beyond what is signified by the diplomatic expression "in principle." Considering the disparity in strength, wealth, and prestige between the northern country and its southern fellows, suggestions of the sort could be made practicable only by letting the United States do whatever it might think needful to accomplish the objects which it sought. Obviously the Hispanic nations, singly or collectively, would hardly venture to take any such action within the borders of the United States itself, if, for example, it failed to maintain what, in their opinion, was "a republican form of government." A full acceptance of the plan accordingly would have amounted to a recognition of American overlordship, and this they were naturally not disposed to admit.

The common perils and duties confronting the Americas as a result of the Great War, however, made close coöperation between the Hispanic republics and the United States up to a certain point indispensable. Toward that transatlantic struggle the attitude of all the nations of the New World at the outset was substantially the same. Though strongly sympathetic on the whole with the "Allies" and notably with France, the southern countries nevertheless declared their neutrality. More than that, they tried to convert neutrality into a Pan-American policy, instead of regarding it as an official attitude to be adopted by the republics separately. Thus when the conflict overseas began to injure the rights of neutrals, Argentina and other nations urged that the countries of the New World jointly agree to declare that direct maritime commerce between American lands should be considered as "inter-American coastwise trade," and that the merchant ships engaged in it, whatever the flag under which they sailed, should be looked upon as neutral. Though the South American countries failed to enlist the support of their northern neighbor in this bold departure from international precedent, they found some compensation for their disappointment in the closer commercial and financial relations which they established with the United States.

Because of the dependence of the Hispanic nations, and especially those of the southern group, on the intimacy of their economic ties with the belligerents overseas, they suffered from the ravages of the struggle more perhaps than other lands outside of

Europe. Negotiations for prospective loans were dropped. Industries were suspended, work on public improvements was checked, and commerce brought almost to a standstill. As the revenues fell off and ready money became scarce, drastic measures had to be devised to meet the financial strain. For the protection of credit, bank holidays were declared, stock exchanges were closed, *moratoria* were set up in nearly all the countries, taxes and duties were increased, radical reductions in expenditure were undertaken, and in a few cases large quantities of paper money were issued.

With the European market thus wholly or partially cut off, the Hispanic republics were forced to supply the consequent shortage with manufactured articles and other goods from the United States and to send thither their raw materials in exchange. To their northern neighbor they had to turn also for pecuniary aid. A Pan-American financial conference was held at Washington in 1915, and an international high commission was appointed to carry its recommendations into effect. Gradually most of the Hispanic countries came to show a favorable trade balance. Then, as the war drew into its fourth year, several of them even began to enjoy great prosperity.

That Pan-Americanism had not meant much more than coöperation for economic ends seemed evident when, on April 6, 1917, the United States declared war on Germany. Instead of following spontaneously in the wake of their great northern neighbor, the Hispanic republics were divided by conflicting currents of opinion and hesitated as to their proper course of procedure. While a majority of them expressed approval of what the United States had done, and while Uruguay for its part asserted that "no American country, which in defense of its own rights should find itself in a state of war with nations of other continents, would be treated as a belligerent," Mexico veered almost to the other extreme by proposing that the republics of America agree to lay an embargo on the shipment of munitions to the warring powers.

As a matter of fact, only seven out of the nineteen Hispanic nations saw fit to imitate the example set by their northern neighbor and to declare war on Germany. These were Cuba — in view of its "duty toward the United States,"— Panamá, Guatemala, Brazil, Honduras, Nicaragua, and Costa Rica. Since the Dominican Republic at the time was under American military control, it was not in a position to choose its course. Four countries — Ecuador, Peru, Bolivia, and Uruguay — broke off diplomatic relations with Germany. The other seven republics — Mexico, Salvador, Colombia, Venezuela, Chile, Argentina, and Paraguay — continued their formal neutrality. In spite of a disclosure made by the United States of insulting and threatening utterances on the part of the German *chargé d'affaires* in Argentina, which led to popular outbreaks at the capital and induced the national Congress to declare in favor of a severance of diplomatic relations with that functionary's Government, the President of the republic stood firm in his resolution to maintain neutrality. If Pan-Americanism had ever involved the idea of political coöperation among the nations of the New World, it broke down just when it might have served the greatest of purposes. Even the "A B C" combination itself had apparently been shattered.

A century and more had now passed since the Spanish and Portuguese peoples of the New World had achieved their independence. Eighteen political children of various sizes and stages of advancement, or backwardness, were born of Spain in America, and one acknowledged the maternity of

Portugal. Big Brazil has always maintained the happiest relations with the little mother in Europe, who still watches with pride the growth of her strapping youngster. Between Spain and her descendants, however, animosity endured for many years after they had thrown off the parental yoke. Yet of late, much has been done on both sides to render the relationship cordial. The graceful act of Spain in sending the much-beloved Infanta Isabel to represent her in Argentina and Chile at the celebration of the centennial anniversary of their cry for independence, and to wish them Godspeed on their onward journey, was typical of the yearning of the mother country for her children overseas, despite the lapse of years and political ties. So, too, her ablest men of intellect have striven nobly and with marked success to revive among them a sense of filial affection and gratitude for all that Spain contributed to mold the mind and heart of her kindred in distant lands. On their part, the Hispanic Americans have come to a clearer consciousness of the fact that on the continents of the New World there are two distinct types of civilization, with all that each connotes of differences in race, psychology, tradition, language, and custom — their own, and that represented by the United States. Appreciative though the southern countries are of their northern neighbor, they cling nevertheless to their heritage from Spain and Portugal in whatever seems conducive to the maintenance of their own ideals of life and thought.

represented by the United States. Appreciative though the southern countries are of their northern neighbor, they cling nevertheless to their heritage from Spain and Portugal in whatever seems conducive to the maintenance of their own ideals of life and thought.

BIBLIOGRAPHICAL NOTE

For anything like a detailed study of the history of the Hispanic nations of America, obviously one must consult works written in Spanish and Portuguese. There are many important books, also, in French and German; but, with few exceptions, the recommendations for the general reader will be limited to accounts in English.

A very useful outline and guide to recent literature on the subject is W. W. Pierson, Jr., *A Syllabus of Latin-American History* (Chapel Hill, North Carolina, 1917). A brief introduction to the history and present aspects of Hispanic American civilization is W. R. Shepherd, *Latin America* (New York, 1914). The best general accounts of the Spanish and Portuguese colonial systems will be found in Charles de Lannoy and Herman van der Linden, *Histoire de l'Expansion Coloniale des Peuples Européens: Portugal et Espagne* (Brussels and Paris, 1907), and Kurt Simon, *Spanien und Portugal als See und Kolonialmächte* (Hamburg, 1913). For the Spanish colonial régime alone, E. G. Bourne, *Spain in America* (New York, 1904) is excellent. The situation in southern South America toward the close of Spanish rule is well described in Bernard Moses, *South America on the Eve of Emancipation* (New York, 1908). Among contemporary accounts of that period, Alexander von

Humboldt and Aimé Bonpland, *Personal Narrative of Travels to the Equinoctial Regions of America*, 3 vols. (London, 1881); Alexander von Humboldt, *Political Essay on the Kingdom of New Spain*, 4 vols. (London, 1811–1822); and F. R. J. de Pons, *Travels in South America*, 2 vols. (London, 1807), are authoritative, even if not always easy to read.

On the wars of independence, see the scholarly treatise by W. S. Robertson, *Rise of the Spanish-American Republics as Told in the Lives of their Liberators* (New York, 1918); Bartolomé Mitre, *The Emancipation of South America* (London, 1893) — a condensed translation of the author's *Historia de San Martín*, and wholly favorable to that patriot; and F. L. Petre, *Simón Bolívar* (London, 1910) — impartial at the expense of the imagination. Among the numerous contemporary accounts, the following will be found serviceable: W. D. Robinson, *Memoirs of the Mexican Revolution* (Philadelphia, 1820); J. R. Poinsett, *Notes on Mexico* (London, 1825); H. M. Brackenridge, *Voyage to South America*, 2 vols. (London, 1820); W. B. Stevenson, *Historical and Descriptive Narrative of Twenty Years' Residence in South America*, 3 vols. (London, 1825); J. Miller, *Memoirs of General Miller in the Service of the Republic of Peru*, 2 vols. (London, 1828); H. L. V. Ducoudray Holstein, *Memoirs of Simón Bolívar*, 2 vols. (London, 1830), and John Armitage, *History of Brazil*, 2 vols. (London, 1836).

The best books on the history of the republics as a whole since the attainment of independence, and written from an Hispanic American viewpoint, are F. García Calderón, *Latin America, its Rise and Progress* (New York, 1913), and M. de Oliveira Lima, *The*

Evolution of Brazil Compared with that of Spanish and Anglo-Saxon America (Stanford University, California, 1914). The countries of Central America are dealt with by W. H. Koebel, *Central America* (New York, 1917), and of South America by T. C. Dawson, *The South American Republics*, 2 vols. (New York, 1903–1904), and C. E. Akers, *History of South America* (London, 1912), though in a manner that often confuses rather than enlightens.

Among the histories and descriptions of individual countries, arranged in alphabetical order, the following are probably the most useful to the general reader: W. A. Hirst, *Argentina* (New York, 1910); Paul Walle, *Bolivia* (New York, 1914); Pierre Denis, *Brazil* (New York, 1911); G. F. S. Elliot, *Chile* (New York, 1907); P. J. Eder, *Colombia* (New York, 1913); J. B. Calvo, *The Republic of Costa Rica* (Chicago, 1890); A. G. Robinson, *Cuba, Old and New* (New York, 1915); Otto Schoenrich, *Santo Domingo* (New York, 1918); C. R. Enock, *Ecuador* (New York, 1914); C. R. Enock, *Mexico* (New York, 1909); W. H. Koebel, *Paraguay* (New York, 1917); C. R. Enock, *Peru* (New York, 1910); W. H. Koebel, *Uruguay* (New York, 1911), and L. V. Dalton, *Venezuela* (New York, 1912). Of these, the books by Robinson and Eder, on Cuba and Colombia, respectively, are the most readable and reliable.

For additional bibliographical references see *South America* and the articles on individual countries in *The Encyclopædia Britannica*, 11th edition, and in Marrion Wilcox and G. E. Rines, *Encyclopedia of Latin America* (New York, 1917).

Of contemporary or later works descriptive of the life

and times of eminent characters in the history of the Hispanic American republics since 1830, a few may be taken as representative. Rosas: J. A. King, *Twenty-four Years in the Argentine Republic* (London, 1846), and Woodbine Parish, *Buenos Ayres and the Provinces of the Rio de la Plata* (London, 1852). Francia: J. R. Rengger, *Reign of Dr. Joseph Gaspard Roderick* [!] *de Francia in Paraguay* (London, 1827); J. P. and W. P. Robertson, *Letters on South America*, 3 vols. (London, 1843), and E. L. White, *El Supremo*, a novel (New York, 1916). Santa Anna: Waddy Thompson, *Recollections of Mexico* (New York, 1846), and F. E. Ingles, Calderón de la Barca, *Life in Mexico* (London, 1852). Juárez: U. R. Burke, *Life of Benito Juárez* (London, 1894). Solano López: T. J. Hutchinson, *Paraná; with Incidents of the Paraguayan War and South American Recollections* (London, 1868); George Thompson, *The War in Paraguay* (London, 1869); R. F. Burton, *Letters from the Battle-fields of Paraguay* (London, 1870), and C. A. Washburn, *The History of Paraguay*, 2 vols. (Boston, 1871). Pedro II: J. C. Fletcher and D. P. Kidder, *Brazil and the Brazilians* (Boston, 1879), and Frank Bennett, *Forty Years in Brazil* (London, 1914). García Moreno: Frederick Hassaurek, *Four Years among Spanish Americans* (New York, 1867). Guzmán Blanco: C. D. Dance, *Recollections of Four Years in Venezuela* (London, 1876). Díaz: James Creelman, *Díaz, Master of Mexico* (New York, 1911). Balmaceda: M. H. Hervey, *Dark Days in Chile* (London, 1891–1892). Carranza: L. Gutiérrez de Lara and Edgcumb Pinchon, *The Mexican People: their Struggle for Freedom* (New York, 1914).

INDEX

AN OUTLINE OF THE PLAN OF THE CHRONICLES OF AMERICA

The fifty titles of the Series fall into eight topical sequences or groups, each with a dominant theme of its own—

I. *The Morning of America*

TIME: 1492-1763

THE theme of the first sequence is the struggle of nations for the possession of the New World. The mariners of four European kingdoms—Spain, Portugal, France, and England—are intent upon the discovery of a new route to Asia. They come upon the American continent which blocks the way. Spain plants colonies in the south, lured by gold. France, in pursuit of the fur trade, plants colonies in the north. Englishmen, in search of homes and of a wider freedom, occupy the Atlantic seaboard. These Englishmen come in time to need the land into which the French have penetrated by way of the St. Lawrence and the Great Lakes, and a mighty struggle between the two nations takes place in the wilderness, ending in the expulsion of the French. This sequence comprises ten volumes:

1. THE RED MAN'S CONTINENT, *by Ellsworth Huntington*
2. THE SPANISH CONQUERORS, *by Irving Berdine Richman*
3. ELIZABETHAN SEA-DOGS, *by William Wood*
4. CRUSADERS OF NEW FRANCE, *by William Bennett Munro*
5. PIONEERS OF THE OLD SOUTH, *by Mary Johnston*
6. THE FATHERS OF NEW ENGLAND, *by Charles M. Andrews*
7. DUTCH AND ENGLISH ON THE HUDSON, *by Maud Wilder Goodwin*
8. THE QUAKER COLONIES, *by Sydney G. Fisher*
9. COLONIAL FOLKWAYS, *by Charles M. Andrews*
10. THE CONQUEST OF NEW FRANCE, *by George M. Wrong*

II. *The Winning of Independence*

TIME: 1763-1815

The French peril has passed, and the great territory between the Alleghanies and the Mississippi is now open to the Englishmen on the seaboard, with no enemy to contest their right of way except the Indian. But the question arises whether these Englishmen in the New World shall submit to political dictation from the King and Parliament of England. To decide this question the War of the Revolution is fought; the Union is born: and the second war with England follows. Seven volumes:

11. THE EVE OF THE REVOLUTION, *by Carl Becker*
12. WASHINGTON AND HIS COMRADES IN ARMS, *by George M. Wrong*
13. THE FATHERS OF THE CONSTITUTION, *by Max Farrand*
14. WASHINGTON AND HIS COLLEAGUES, *by Henry Jones Ford*
15. JEFFERSON AND HIS COLLEAGUES, *by Allen Johnson*
16. JOHN MARSHALL AND THE CONSTITUTION, *by Edward S. Corwin*
17. THE FIGHT FOR A FREE SEA, *by Ralph D. Paine*

III. *The Vision of the West*

TIME: 1750-1890

The theme of the third sequence is the American frontier—the conquest of the continent from the Alleghanies to the Pacific Ocean. The story covers nearly a century and a half, from the first crossing of the Alleghanies by the backwoodsmen of Pennsylvania, Virginia, and the Carolinas (about 1750) to the heyday of the cowboy on the Great Plains in the latter part of the nineteenth century. This is the marvelous tale of the greatest migrations in history, told in nine volumes as follows:

18. PIONEERS OF THE OLD SOUTHWEST, *by Constance Lindsay Skinner*
19. THE OLD NORTHWEST, *by Frederic Austin Ogg*
20. THE REIGN OF ANDREW JACKSON, *by Frederic Austin Ogg*
21. THE PATHS OF INLAND COMMERCE, *by Archer B. Hulbert*
22. ADVENTURERS OF OREGON, by *Constance Lindsay Skinner*
23. THE SPANISH BORDERLANDS, *by Herbert E. Bolton*
24. TEXAS AND THE MEXICAN WAR, *by Nathaniel W. Stephenson*
25. THE FORTY-NINERS, *by Stewart Edward White*
26. THE PASSING OF THE FRONTIER, *by Emerson Hough*

IV. *The Storm of Secession*

TIME: 1830-1876

The curtain rises on the gathering storm of secession. The theme of the fourth sequence is the preservation of the Union, which carries with it the extermination of slavery. Six volumes as follows:

27. THE COTTON KINGDOM, *by William E. Dodd*
28. THE ANTI-SLAVERY CRUSADE, *by Jesse Macy*
29. ABRAHAM LINCOLN AND THE UNION, *by Nathaniel W. Stephenson*
30. THE DAY OF THE CONFEDERACY, *by Nathaniel W. Stephenson*
31. CAPTAINS OF THE CIVIL WAR, *by William Wood*
32. THE SEQUEL OF APPOMATTOX, *by Walter Lynwood Fleming*

V. *The Intellectual Life*

Two volumes follow on the higher national life, telling of the nation's great teachers and interpreters:

33. THE AMERICAN SPIRIT IN EDUCATION, *by Edwin E. Slosson*
34. THE AMERICAN SPIRIT IN LITERATURE, *by Bliss Perry*

VI. *The Epic of Commerce and Industry*

The sixth sequence is devoted to the romance of industry and business, and the dominant theme is the transformation caused by the inflow of immigrants and the development and utilization of mechanics on a great scale. The long age of muscular power has passed, and the era of mechanical power has brought with it a new kind of civilization. Eight volumes:

35. OUR FOREIGNERS, *by Samuel P. Orth*
36. THE OLD MERCHANT MARINE, *by Ralph D. Paine*
37. THE AGE OF INVENTION, *by Holland Thompson*
38. THE RAILROAD BUILDERS, *by John Moody*
39. THE AGE OF BIG BUSINESS, *by Burton J. Hendrick*
40. THE ARMIES OF LABOR, *by Samuel P. Orth*
41. THE MASTERS OF CAPITAL, *by John Moody*
42. THE NEW SOUTH, *by Holland Thompson*

VII. *The Era of World Power*

The seventh sequence carries on the story of government and diplomacy and political expansion from the Reconstruction (1876) to the present day, in six volumes:

43. THE BOSS AND THE MACHINE, *by Samuel P. Orth*
44. THE CLEVELAND ERA, *by Henry Jones Ford*
45. THE AGRARIAN CRUSADE, *by Solon J. Buck*
46. THE PATH OF EMPIRE, *by Carl Russell Fish*
47. THEODORE ROOSEVELT AND HIS TIMES, *by Harold Howland*
48. WOODROW WILSON AND THE WORLD WAR, *by Charles Seymour*

VIII. *Our Neighbors*

Now to round out the story of the continent, the Hispanic peoples on the south and the Canadians on the north are taken up where they were dropped further back in the Series, and these peoples are followed down to the present day:

49. THE CANADIAN DOMINION, *by Oscar D. Skelton*
50. THE HISPANIC NATIONS OF THE NEW WORLD, *by William R. Shepherd*

The Chronicles of America is thus a great synthesis, giving a new projection and a new interpretation of American History. These narratives are works of real scholarship, for every one is written after an exhaustive examination of the sources. Many of them contain new facts; some of them —such as those by Howland, Seymour, and Hough—are founded on intimate personal knowledge. But the originality of the Series lies, not chiefly in new facts, but rather in new ideas and new combinations of old facts.

The General Editor of the Series is Dr. Allen Johnson, Chairman of the Department of History of Yale University, and the entire work has been planned, prepared, and published under the control of the Council's Committee on Publications of Yale University.

YALE UNIVERSITY PRESS

143 ELM STREET, NEW HAVEN

522 FIFTH AVENUE, NEW YORK